DESIGNING EFFECTIVE ORGANIZATIONS

Wiley Series On
ORGANIZATIONAL ASSESSMENT AND CHANGE

Designing Effective Organizations: The Sociotechnical Systems Perspective

William A. Pasmore, Ph.D.
Case Western Reserve University

WILEY

John Wiley & Sons

New York • Chichester • Brisbane • Toronto • Singapore

Library of Congress Cataloging in Publication Data:

Pasmore, William A.
    Designing effective organizations: the sociotechnical systems
perspective / William A. Pasmore.
        p.   cm. –
(Wiley series on organizational assessment and change)
    ISBN 0-471-88785-4
        1. Organization.   2. Organizational effectiveness.
3. Social systems.   I. Title.   II. Series.
HM131.P3426   1988
302.3'5 – dc 19   87-29521
                                                       CIP

Printed in the United States of America
10 9 8 7 6 5 4 3 2 1

To Eric Trist, who created the vision;
Don King, who helped me to see it;
and Jack Sherwood, who helped me to share it with others.

Series Preface

The ORGANIZATIONAL ASSESSMENT AND CHANGE SERIES is concerned with informing and furthering contemporary debate on the effectiveness of work organizations and the quality of life they provide for their members. Of particular relevance is the adaptation of work organizations to changing social aspirations and economic constraints. There has been a phenomenal growth of interest in the quality of work life and productivity in recent years. Issues that not long ago were the quiet concern of a few academics and a few leaders in unions and management have become issues of broader public interest. They have intruded upon broadcast media prime time, lead newspaper and magazine columns, the houses of Congress, and the board rooms of both firms and unions.

A thorough discussion of what organizations should be like and how they can be improved must comprehend many issues. Some are concerned with basic moral and ethical questions—What is the responsibility of an organization to its employees?—What, after all, is a "good job"? —How should it be decided that some might benefit from and others pay for gains in the quality of work life? —Should there be a public policy on the matter? Yet others are concerned with the strategies and tactics of bringing about changes in organizational life, the advocates of alternative approaches being numerous, vocal, and controversial; and still others are concerned with the task of measurement and assessment on grounds that the choices to be made by leaders, the assessment of consequences, and the bargaining of equities must be informed by reliable, comprehensive, and relevant information of kinds not now readily available.

The WILEY SERIES ON ORGANIZATIONAL ASSESSMENT AND CHANGE is concerned with all aspects of the debate on how organizations should be managed, changed, and controlled. It includes books on organizational effectiveness, and the study of organizational changes that represent new approaches to organization design and process. The volumes in the series have in common a concern with work organizations, a focus on change and the dynamics of change, an assumption that diverse social and personal interests need to be taken into account in discussions of organizational effectiveness, and a view that concrete cases and quantitative data are essential ingredients in a lucid debate. As such, these books consider a broad but integrated set of issues and ideas. They are intended to be read by managers, union officials, researchers, consultants, policy makers, students, and others seriously concerned with organizational assessment and change.

EDWARD E. LAWLER, III
STANLEY E. SEASHORE

Ann Arbor, Michigan
January 1985

Preface

Interest in sociotechnical systems design has grown steadily during the past four decades. In this country, the pioneering work begun in the late 1960s and early 1970s by General Foods at its Topeka, Kansas plant and Procter & Gamble at its Lima, Ohio facility was the source of inspiration for hundreds of manufacturing and later nonmanufacturing experiments. But the experimentation began long before, in England, India, and Norway during the 1950s, by members of the Tavistock Institute in London in conjunction with the British coal mining industry, an Indian weaving firm, and a Norwegian metalworking company. Since then, no other method of organization development has proven as successful in improving bottom-line organizational effectiveness while also paying attention to human values. The pressure to improve productivity is not new, nor is it likely to disappear anytime soon. In an evermore competitive world, managers are considering sociotechnical systems design as an approach to stay ahead in the race.

My own decision to write about the sociotechnical systems approach came after years of struggling to understand it, first as a student and later as a consultant. I found its wisdom to be buried in obscure, unpublished documents and scattered over several books and many scholarly journals, none of which seemed to present a coherent gestalt of the entire paradigm. Some of the most important work was written in obtuse jargon and general systems theory terminology, most of which I have tried to avoid incorporating here. My intent was to create a thoughtful but readable account of the theory and practice of the sociotechnical systems approach, so that many others could grasp its significance and usefulness in revitalizing organizations.

As has been said many times, writing a book is a solitary but not autonomous undertaking. Many of the ideas here belong to others who have helped develop the sociotechnical systems paradigm and I have tried to be consistent in giving credit where it is due. I have also been helped immeasurably by the input and support from my friends and colleagues, whom I now thank.

First, my thanks to Stan Seashore and Ed Lawler for encouraging me to write this book and include it in their series on organizational assessment and change. I appreciate their comments on an earlier draft of the manuscript and their patience as I took their comments to heart in revising it. The product is much better, thanks to their thoughful criticism. Thanks, too, to John Mahaney, my editor at Wiley.

The list of people who contributed to the evolution of my thinking here begins with Donald King, my mentor at Purdue. It was his teaching and willingness to involve me in sociotechnical systems consulting with him that started me on my journey. Jack Sherwood, whom I also met while at Purdue, has been a continuing source of support in helping me to publish and disseminate information about the sociotechnical systems approach. His comments on several of the chapters included here and his lasting friendship are greatly appreciated.

My thinking evolved substantially in the years since I have been at Case Western Reserve, largely because of discussions and collaboration with my colleagues and students. Some who have contributed directly to my thinking in this book include David Cooperrider, Carole Francis, Frank Friedlander, Jeff Haldeman, Marty Kaplan, Barry Morris, Jean Neumann, Jeff Petee, Abraham Shani, and Suresh Srivastva.

I also owe thanks to the many clients who provided me with the opportunity to try my ideas out in their organizations. Among them are Don Septor and Dale Sadler at General Foods; John Mietus and Colonel James McMurrer in the U.S. Army; Dr. George Hoffman and Richard Bastian at the Cleveland Clinic; Phil Ensor, Mike Burns, Kathy Gurley, Fred Kovac, and Tom Ford at Goodyear; Jack Wilkens, Dave Walsh, Ed Bretschneider, Satish Agrawal, and Warren Dillman at Polaroid; Roz Eichhorn at Syncrude and Larry Ferretti at General Electric. I've teamed up with Al Fitz on a couple of these projects, and am grateful for what he has taught me about consulting, for his optimistic view of the world and for his friendship.

Retta Holdorf deserves thanks for her willingness to turn my chicken scratches into readable manuscript pages on several chapters; thanks also to the editors at Wiley who helped to get the manuscript into shape.

Finally, my thanks go to my wife Carol for all the times she listened, watched, and encouraged me as I gave my attention to this book instead of to her. My admiration for her patience and understanding continues to grow, as does my love.

WILLIAM A. PASMORE

Cleveland, Ohio
March, 1988

Contents

DESIGNING EFFECTIVE ORGANIZATIONS

CHAPTER ONE

Introduction

Effective organizations are those which produce excellent results by any measure of costs, quality, or efficiency while simultaneously enhancing the energy and commitment of organizational members to the success of the enterprise. This book is about the design of effective organizations. The need to discover more effective ways of organizing has become increasingly apparent. Whether one reads the popular press or scholarly journals, the message is the same: American organizations are in trouble as they face increasing pressures stemming from international competition, governmental regulation, and their own international competition, governmental regulation and their own internal inefficiencies. The case for improvement hardly needs to be made again; yet the answer to the question, "What can be done?" is still evasive.

The sociotechnical systems approach to organizational design has proven successful in organizations throughout the world for the past 35 years (Pasmore, Francis, Haldeman & Shani, 1978; Taylor, 1975). Its success is attributable both to the theory of organizations upon which it is based and to the unique methods which have been developed to apply this theory to organizational redesign. The sociotechnical systems perspective considers every organization to be made up of people (the social system) using tools, techniques and knowledge (the technical system) to produce goods or services valued by customers (who are part of the organization's external environment). How well the social and technical systems are designed *with respect to one another and with respect to the demands of the external environment* determines to a large extent how effective the organization will be. Thus, every organization is a sociotechnical system, but not every organization is designed using the principles and techniques that have come to be a part of the sociotechnical systems approach.

1

Researchers have discovered that some ways of organizing are more effective than others. Beginning with the founding work of Trist and his colleagues at the Tavistock Institute in London (Trist & Bamforth, 1951; Rice, 1958; Trist, Higgin, Murray & Pollock, 1963) nearly four decades of research have confirmed that how organizations are designed impacts both their performance and the satisfaction of their members. In his initial study of the British coal mining industry, Trist concluded that the behavior of organizational members was so tightly coupled to the way work was designed that the human system could not be understood without also understanding the technical system. Trist et al. (1963) further concluded that *changing* the design of the technical system would affect the social system and vice-versa. The title of their book, *Organizational Choice*, reflected their understanding that even in organizations utilizing the same technology, different work arrangements were possible.

In contrast to approaches to organizational design which focus on either the social system or the technical system exclusively, the sociotechnical systems approach holds that the most effective arrangements will be those that integrate the demands of both. Emery (1959) referred to this dual concern with social and technical systems as *joint optimization*; peak performance can only be achieved when the needs of both systems are met.

Furthermore, Trist et al. (1963) recognized that organizations must be thought of as *open systems*, borrowing from Bertalanffy's (1940) development of general systems theory in biology. The open systems perspective holds that every living organism depends upon its environment for inputs which allow it to survive. If the flow of inputs is interrupted, the organism will eventually cease to exist. Organizations assure their flow of inputs by providing goods or services which individuals or other organizations desire; in exchange for providing these goods or services, the organization obtains capital which can be used for the acquisition of additional inputs. The more efficient the conversion process (the fewer inputs used to produce outputs) the healthier the organization will be. Over time, if the organization can retain more inputs than it requires to produce outputs, it will develop a reserve against changes in its environment which might otherwise threaten its survival. In simple business terminology, the more competitive the organization becomes, the more likely it is to survive and prosper.

These perspectives appear straightforward—perhaps even obvious. Yet they helped sociotechnical systems theorists to focus attention on dynamic processes within organizations and between organizations and their environments that had until that time been largely ignored. The sociotechnical systems perspective insists that whatever decisions are made about organizational design should meet the demands of the external environment as well as the internal social and technical systems. Internal measures of success are viewed as insufficient predictors of organizational survival; the external environment is the ultimate judge of design effectiveness. If consumers of goods or services, providers of capital, or providers of labor withdraw their support, no amount of improvement by internal standards will prevent catastrophe.

As obvious as it seems, the open systems perspective continues to receive less attention than it deserves. Organizations persist in ignoring or downplaying the very real threats to their survival posed by their environments. One automaker boasts that it offers the "Best-built American cars," in an attempt to deny the ready availability of better-built foreign products; a defense contractor withdraws its multi-million dollar entry into the fighter jet market when it realizes that the government has no intention of purchasing its product; a high-tech firm depletes its resources pursuing the independent development of a new product which turns out to be much more expensive and less versatile than one made by its chief competitor. Open systems thinking forces a reality test of organizational effectiveness against external criteria; self-delusions ("Ours is the best product"; "Our organizational design isn't the problem") are shattered by the abrasive contact of the organization with its environment. The open systems perspective demands that we reconsider the nature of organizations and their evolution; as we do, new design possibilities emerge.

The Nature of Organizations

The creation of an organization is a complex undertaking, during which many decisions are made without complete information (Bartunek & Louis, 1988; Greiner, 1972). Often, the intuition of the founders leads them to arbitrary choices of what markets to enter, what technology to use in producing goods, who to hire, and how to organize. While making such choices, the founders recognize the uncertainty they are facing and view initial decisions as experimental and subject to revision in the face of actual experience. Over time, however, the arbitrariness of these decisions is often forgotten. As the organization begins to function, ways are found to make the decisions work rather than to challenge them. Through trial and error, standard modes of operation develop. At the same time, organizational members begin to understand how the organization will operate and their place within it. Decisions and procedures become familiar; annoying discrepancies between what was envisioned and what exists become accepted as "Just the way it is."

As more time passes, members become invested in their roles and the security those roles provide. Roles provide a sense of identity, both within and outside of the organization. Lines and boxes on organizational charts that were originally viewed as experimental now take on special meaning as they are associated with specific individuals and the relationships among them.

As people strive to make the organization successful, they gradually come to depend on others in the organization to provide them with support in specific ways. To enhance the predictability of these relationships, behaviors are formalized through employment contracts, rules, policies, and procedures. Once written, these formal guidelines become difficult to challenge, since they represent both security and historical success to the parties affected by them.

Long after the founders have departed, people continue to uphold the decisions they once made, forgetting that the founders' decisions were arbitrary. The intentions of the founders are no longer directly accessible; they must be inferred from the structural legacy left behind. To question the structure is to question the wisdom of the founders and to challenge everything that has allowed the organization to survive. The organization may become reified, calcified, and unresponsive to changes in its environment. "Don't fix it if it ain't broken" becomes a familiar chant. Ultimately, the success of traditional arrangements may become the organization's undoing, as necessary changes are avoided in order to preserve the status quo.

To design organizations that are effective and will remain adaptive to their environments, historical success must be mistrusted (Weick, 1979), and the true nature of organizations must be understood. First, it must be recognized that organizations have no mental or physical properties of their own, independent of those who create them and bestow them with meaning. When we search for tangible manifestations of organizations, we find buildings, capital, equipment, and people who are co-located in time and space; we notice that there are organizational charts, advertising slogans, and even organizational cultures. But none of these *are* the organization.

Organizations are legal fictions, created for the basic purpose of accomplishing tasks that individuals could not accomplish by working alone (Barnard, 1938). Organizations exist in the form of agreements among people. They do not have independent minds and cannot act in ways which are contrary to the wishes of their members. They do only what their members want and are nothing more than their members make them.

When this is forgotten, people in organizations find it difficult to discard rules which are no longer appropriate; to unlearn behaviors which have become dysfunctional, to leave old markets and enter new arenas, to innovate, to adapt, to embrace technological advances, to recognize changes in the needs of their members, and to experiment with new ways of organizing. No matter how permanent they might seem, organizations are at best temporary solutions to ill-defined problems. They are responses to specific circumstances based upon imperfect information and unclear desires; they are alliances among people in the face of uncertainty. Most importantly, they are capable of being transformed at will by their members.

If organizations are agreements among people, it follows that changing the nature of the agreements changes the nature of organizations. If agreements are good—meaning that individuals are fully committed to helping the organization succeed, are able to work together effectively, and are provided with the proper tools and resources—the organization is more likely to be adaptable and to survive. When agreements are poor, individuals feel compelled to protect their own interests instead of being concerned with the success of the organization as a whole. Structures interfere with cooperation and effective task performance; tools are inappropriate for the tasks being performed; and products fail to meet market demands.

Thus, for an organization to introduce changes in the design of work, it must change agreements among people; but because agreements are vested with historical meaning, attempts at change often meet with resistance. Therefore, in addition to recognizing the need to change, organizations must also pay attention to the *process* of changing. New agreements must be understood and accepted before they result in improved organizational effectiveness.

Summary

To use the ideas and approaches outlined in this book, the reader must understand the assumptions about organizations which underlie the sociotechnical systems perspective. The first of these is that while organizational design is not always completely rational, it is choiceful. Many designs are possible and some are superior. Organizational design begins with organizational creation and evolves over time; to the extent that this evolution reflects the real demands of the external environment and moves closer to the joint optimization of the organization's social and technical systems, survival is more likely.

Second, it is assumed that organizations are agreements among people and that changes in the organization will affect these agreements and vice-versa. Therefore, in addition to determining which changes in design will be most effective, it is especially important to focus attention on the process of change itself.

This book reflects these two assumptions in its review of sociotechnical systems theory and its exploration of methods of organizational analysis and change. Chapter 2 considers organizations as open systems, outlining important propositions concerning the influence of the environment on organizational design. Chapter 3 addresses the social system of the organization, and Chapter 4 the technical system. Chapter 5 reviews the principles of sociotechnical systems design which guide the integration of social and technical systems in the context of the environment. Chapter 6 focuses on the sociotechnical systems change process, building upon the analytical techniques which are discussed in the earlier chapters. Chapter 7 discusses the unique role of leaders in innovative sociotechnical systems, and Chapter 8 provides some further thoughts about the future of organizations and of the sociotechnical systems paradigm.

CHAPTER TWO

The Environment

All organizations exist in the context of other organizations and larger systems: systems of government, systems of nations, ecological systems, transportation systems, systems of cultural beliefs, systems of trade, monetary systems, and the solar system, to name a few. It is convenient to speak of the totality of systems surrounding and influencing a focal organization as that organization's environment, realizing, of course, that the environment of any organization is immensely complex and continuously changing.

In the face of this complexity, it is tempting to avoid the challenge of comprehending the environment altogether. Historically, some organizations have followed just this course—only to discover that the penalties for environmental ignorance are severe. The American Buggy Whip Company continued to manufacture buggy whips after the advent of the horseless carriage; the Penn Central Railroad refused to acknowledge the arrival of alternative modes of shipping transportation; Sweda plowed the company's assets into the mechanical calculator market despite the appearance of electronic calculators; and U.S. automakers failed to take Japanese competition seriously.

The reasons why organizations ignore their environments despite such great peril have been explored elsewhere (March & Simon, 1958; Weick, 1979). Our concern is with the influence of the environment on organizational design. Failure to design the organization to fit with the environment is as dangerous as totally ignoring the environment; while the ultimate effects of a mismatch between the design and the environment are not always immediately obvious, they are usually severe.

The environment plays the paradoxical roles of providing an organization with resources needed for survival while acting as the final judge of the organization's success. The environment is thus both friend and foe. Organizations seek to reduce their dependence upon their environments in various ways (Thompson, 1967) but can never do so completely. Hence, organizational designs must take the demands of the environment into account while simultaneously seeking to buffer core technologies from environmental influences that threaten survival.

Because the environment is in a constant state of flux, demands are constantly shifting. It follows that for the fit between the organization and environment to remain optimal, the design of the organization also must change continuously. For those who worship stable organizational structures, changes in the environment are easily viewed as *Provocations*. But for those who seize environmental changes as opportunities to gain competitive advantages through organizational redesign, the same environmental changes can be viewed as *Inspirations*. In this chapter we explore the environment as a source of both provocation and inspiration. We consider how the environment is known to organizational members and how they, in turn, help to create it. Then we discuss the implications of the sociotechnical systems perspective of the environment for the design of effective organizations.

The Environment as a Source of Provocation

In 1965, Emery and Trist published an article on the causal texture of organizational environments in which they argued that, "The main problem in the study of organizational change is that the environmental contexts in which organizations exist are themselves changing at an increasing rate and towards increasing complexity" (p. 21). Although written more than 20 years ago, this statement remains an accurate portrayal of the challenge facing designers of modern organizations. Organizational environments have indeed become increasingly complex, moving toward what Emery and Trist described as "turbulent fields," in which the environment is changing independently of organizational actions but in ways that are often threatening to organizational survival.

Some trends in the environment are more apparent now than they were 20 years ago, and have been described by Bell (1973), Toffler (1980), Yankelovich (1982), Naisbitt (1984), and others. These include trends toward greater automation; higher education; increased world interdependencies; the gradual dissolution of stable social structures like the family; increasing competition for scarce resources; less tolerance for authority; a shift from employment in manufacturing industries to employment in service industries; greater concern for the environment; an increasing rate of technological innovation; shifts in population centers and demographic characteristics of the workforce; reduced loyalties to single organizations and increased loyalties to professions;

continued pressures for equality of treatment on the part of women and minorities; and new attitudes toward work.

Other trends are less obvious, but no less critical to the future of organizational design. Examples are: shifts in international trade agreements; the movement toward economic and industrial democracy; the emergence of distinct classes of people not because of sex or race but based upon access to technical knowledge; experimentation in labor-management agreements; and the appearance of innovative and highly successful organizational forms. As a basic tenet, organizational designs should "fit" with the environment (Kotter, 1978), but these rapid and often unpredictable changes make achieving the proper fit difficult. The environment simply won't stand still long enough to be fully understood. Changes introduced into social and technical systems within an organization by the environment make the quest for joint optimization not unlike the search for the holy grail. In the technological arena, automation, robotics, CAD-CAM, flexible manufacturing systems, automated inventory handling systems, information systems and related advancements are rapidly displacing conventional tools and systems. These changes carry implications for social systems in areas such as staffing, selection, training, compensation, and supervision. In a rapidly changing world, flexibility may replace joint optimization as a sociotechnical systems design objective.

The environment provides further provocation in the forms of competition and regulation. Competition, particularly competition from abroad, has made it impossible for many U.S. firms to continue business as usual. At the same time, there seems to be a growing recognition among both businessmen and politicians that U.S. firms enter the competitive fray with one hand tied behind their backs by regulations. Regulations add to the drive for efficiency as U.S. manufacturers struggle to compete despite higher fixed costs tied to meeting regulatory guidelines.

In summary, the environment is a harsh teacher which doles out severe penalties for failures to meet its demands. Organizations, while they may seek to limit their dependence on the environment, must recognize that complete independence is impossible. Furthermore, the complexity of the environment dictates that success be achieved in meeting demands on several (often competing) fronts simultaneously. Organizations must stay ahead of the competition technologically, but they must do so while maintaining quality, lowering costs, continuing favorable relations with employees, abiding by regulations, satisfying shareholders, placating creditors, and responding to market fluctuations.

For many organizations, the provocations introduced by the environment have simply become too severe. Some obsolescence is natural but the current rate of demise is startling – with the outlook for the future not much brighter. Clearly, it is no longer sufficient to recognize that changes in the environment are occurring. Survival in the turbulent environment of the nineties and beyond will require proactivity (Ackoff, 1974), which in turn requires that the environment be viewed not as a source of provocation, but instead a fountainhead of inspiration.

Our arguments thus far can be summarized in the following propositions:

> **Proposition 2:1.** The higher the level of environmental provocation, the more likely it is that organizational adaptation will occur.
>
> **Proposition 2:2.** The more complex the environment, the more likely it is that a design will fail to satisfy certain important environmental demands.
>
> **Proposition 2:3.** The more turbulent the environment, the more flexibility should be valued over optimization as a design objective.
>
> **Proposition 2:4.** The more the environment is viewed as a source of provocation, the more adaptation will focus on solving immediate problems versus innovations in organizational design.

The Environment as a Source of Inspiration

While many organizations seem to choke on the demands made by turbulent environments, some thrive in the same situations. Turbulence, by definition, introduces uncertainty into precisely those areas which are most critical to smooth organizational functioning (Emery and Trist, 1965). This "relevant uncertainty" destroys plans, causes product failures, and rewrites the rules by which competitive games are played. When faced with relevant uncertainty, it makes little sense to prepare for the future by returning to actions that were successful in the past.

Organizations that thrive in turbulent environments view each rule broken, each strategy undone, and each product failure as creating opportunities for learning. Turbulent environments assist these organizations in becoming more successful by making success more difficult for their tradition-bound counterparts. Several years ago it was the Japanese who recognized that the environment would assist them in entering U.S. markets. Some U.S. firms caught off-guard by Japanese competitors and unable to adjust their organizational designs to respond quickly to the challenge are only now beginning to recover. Firms such as General Motors, LTV Steel, General Electric, Allen-Bradley, and Xerox have recognized the need to adopt new manufacturing technologies and develop new relations with labor in order to compete in the world market.

Companies that are successful in turbulent environments do more than react to competition; they take steps to transform the environment itself to make it more conducive to their continued well-being. GM, for example, did not merely respond to the Japanese challenge by importing Japanese technology. Instead, actions were taken on several fronts simultaneously. An alliance was struck with Toyota to manufacture some vehicles jointly; at the same time, lobbyists applied pressure on legislators to place tougher quotas on Japanese imports. Meanwhile, GM also used its recent experience in experimenting with sociotechnical systems design to begin planning for the new Saturn Corporation which was given unprecedented autonomy from Detroit to allow it freedom to innovate. The explicit goal of Saturn Corporation is to produce an automobile of world-class quality at a cost which makes it competitive with vehicles manufactured anywhere in the world. It is doubtful that such extreme actions would have been contemplated by GM in the sixties or even the seventies. The environment clearly provoked GM into action. Later, however, the environment became a source of inspiration for GM, and the actions they took are already changing the environment itself in ways that will benefit them in the future.

Similar responses have been triggered in non-manufacturing settings. Citibank, for example, facing increasing competition for commercial customers, used new data processing technology in combination with a new sociotechnical systems design to provide improved customer service (Walters, 1982). In health care, physicians, hospitals, and insurers are finding the environment increasingly provocative. Some are hurting and trying to respond by belt-tightening; the Cleveland Clinic, on the other hand, embarked on a multi-million dollar expansion program to assure itself a predominant position in the transformed health care environment of the future (Cooperrider, 1985). The Clinic did not simply respond; it viewed the environment as a source of inspiration for bold actions it might not have taken otherwise.

Proposition 2:5. Organizations which view the environment as a source of inspiration are more likely to adapt to changes through innovations in design rather than short-run problem solving.

Proposition 2:6. The more turbulent the environment, the more important it is for innovative adaptations to transform the environment as well as the organization.

Proposition 2:7. To effect change in the environment, actions taken by an organization must be at least as powerful as the forces that originally created the environment.

Regardless of the nature of the industry or its environment, historical analysis demonstrates that change will remain the only constant

(Toffler, 1980). Those who wish to design effective organizations must take the environment into account. For optimal success, the environment must also be viewed not as a constraint upon design parameters, but rather as a stimulus for considering new design possibilities. The open systems perspective (Bertalanffy, 1950) has often overlooked the environment as a source of stimulation for innovation. Now open systems theorists and organizational designers must adopt a view of the environment as transitory and shifting, demanding a more strategic interdependence between the organization and its context in which influence occurs in both directions. Organizations must be viewed as capable not only of sensing and responding to the demands of the environment, but also of transforming those demands.

Proposition 2:8. In order to adapt to environmental demands, organizations must first be able to determine that demands exists and to distinguish which require response and which do not.

Proposition 2:9. Responses to environmental demands can take one of two forms: (a) reacting to the demands as they are presented; or (b) transforming the environment so as to eliminate or alter the demands.

How the Environment Is Known

The process through which the environment is comprehended by organizational members is more complex than early open systems theorists imagined. Bertalanffy (1950) in his classic formulation of open systems theory in physics and biology, likened living systems (and by later extrapolation, organizations) to single cells. In this formulation, the survival of a cell depends upon its transactions with its physical environment through precise, continuous chemical reactions. The "challenges" for the cell in this formulation were to: (1) locate itself in an environment capable of sustaining life, and (2) engage in interactions with the environment which would result in the continuing importation of energy. Without this continuous importation of energy, the cell would eventually die, since it was incapable of self-generation of the energy needed to sustain its living processes. This made the cell dependent upon, or "open" to its environment.

While Bertalanffy acknowledged the principle of equifinality, which holds that living systems are capable of engaging in many different behaviors to achieve a desired outcome (like survival), for the most part, he viewed the task of open systems to be responding to their environments rather than creating them. The single cell formulation made the consideration of a system transforming its environment difficult.

Bertalanffy's simplistic view of systems theory was adopted by organizational theorists to expose shortcomings in management practices. Katz and Kahn (1966) argued that organizations are more than teleological structures for accomplishing the purposes of their leaders. They saw organizations as constantly changing to adapt to new conditions encountered in their environments, often in ways contrary to the wishes of organizational leaders:

> The typical models in organizational theorizing concentrate upon principles of internal functioning as if these problems were independent of changes in the environment and as if they did not affect the maintenance of inputs of motivation and morale. Moves toward a tighter integration and coordination are made to ensure stability, when flexibility may be the more important requirement. They are not seen in full perspective as adjusting the system to its environment but as desirable goals within a closed system. In fact, however, every attempt at coordination which is not functionally required may produce a host of new organizational problems (p. 26).

Thus, the open systems perspective, as it was introduced into the organizational design literature, provided an understanding of why designs needed to take the environment into account. It did not, however, view the environment as malleable. The challenges for the manager in the open systems perspective were the same as for the cell — to seek a hospitable environment in which to do business and then to engage in activities conducive to the continued exchange of resources. This view of the manager's role has proven to be overly simplistic.

Two things make the cell formulation difficult to apply to organizational situations. First, organizational environments are more difficult to comprehend than those of single biological cells where contexts can be characterized precisely through physical analyses. In the case of organizational environments, many different, intangible, and sometimes conflicting bits of data must be assimilated before the nature of the environment becomes even slightly more lucid (Friedlander & Pickle, 1967; Pfeffer & Salancik, 1977). We have called this feature of organizational environments *Complexity*. Second, as noted previously, the environments faced by many organizations today are *Turbulent*, meaning that they are changing rapidly and unpredictably. Both the complexity and turbulence of organizational environments makes the challenges of locating hospitable environments and deciding how to engage in exchanges with them extremely difficult, if not at times impossible.

Despite the difficulties involved in comprehending the environment, managers and designers must attempt to do so. The environment, regardless of its levels of complexity and turbulence, remains the final judge of organizational success. As we have learned more about the processes of environmental comprehension, the need to replace simplistic open systems thinking with more realistic ideas about how organizations interact with their environments has become more apparent.

Figure 2-1 depicts the primary steps in the process of environmental comprehensive/adaptation.

Beginning with the basic sociotechnical systems model, we see the organization engaging in continuous transactions with its environment. The primary purpose of these interactions is to maintain the stable flow of inputs the organization needs to survive. If inputs are readily available, meaning that the environment continues to demand the organization's outputs and is willing to exchange inputs for them, interactions may reach a steady state or dynamic homeostasis (Katz & Kahn, 1966). In this state, the basic character of the system remains unchanged even though the system is constantly in motion and minor alterations are taking place within it. Equipment is wearing out, employees are growing older, old inventory is replaced with new inventory, and so forth.

To anticipate the need to replace depreciated assets and to guard against minor shocks introduced by demand fluctuations or input shortages, the steady state system must import slightly more energy than it expends. In this way, the system overcomes small threats to its ability to satisfy environmental demands, and maintains smoother operations. Larger threats to organizational stability require additional

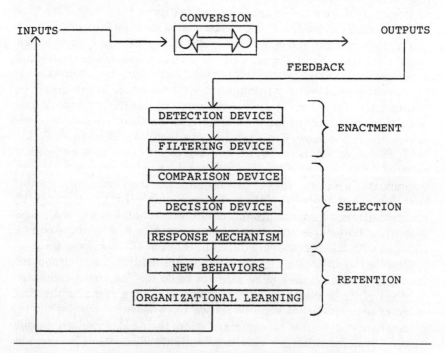

Figure 2-1 The Environmental Feedback Process

slack resources to allow appropriate adjustments to be made (Galbraith, 1977).

Proposition 2:10. Responses to changes in the environment require resources proportionate to the significance of the changes.

Proposition 2:10 implies that when faced with significant threats from the environment, low cost, quick-fix strategies are unlikely to result in successful adaptation. Instead, more comprehensive, long-term, and often more expensive strategies are called for to meet serious challenges. If an organization is skillful at monitoring its environment, small adaptations may preclude the need to engage eventually in major redesign. On the other hand, if an organization is a poor reader of environmental trends, it may find itself faced with the need to make major changes at a time when resources are unavailable. Hence, skills in both comprehending the environment and either responding to or effecting changes in the environment are crucial in maintaining steady state operations.

As indicated in Figure 2-1, the process of recognizing changes in the environment is a complex one, with many opportunities for misinterpretation. First, the challenge in the environment must be detected; this implies that information gathering mechanisms are in place and that scanning activities occur which permit decision makers to take note of environmental perturbations. The form of the detection device can vary from an executive simply reading the *Wall Street Journal* to elaborate open systems planning (Jayaram, 1976) or search conferences (Emery, 1982). An important feature of the detection device is its sensitivity; that is, its ability to capture and reproduce faithfully significant changes in the environment. Because the environments of most organizations are complex and turbulent, simple detection devices may not pick up significant challenges. Using simple detection devices to comprehend such environments is akin to trying to capture the sound of the London Symphony on cheap recording tape. To hear the music as it was actually played, the recording device must be at least as sensitive as the intonations in the music itself.

Proposition 2:11. Environmental sensing devices should be at least as sensitive as the context which needs to be understood.

Proposition 2:12. The more sensitive the environmental detection device, the more challenges will be available for response.

Of course, too much sensitivity in the detection device can quickly lead to data overload and decision paralysis. Automakers in Detroit must separate information critical to competitive decision making from information concerning the price of tea in China. Thus, a filtering device of some sort is required which imposes decision rules on where to pay attention. Sensitive recording equipment may pick up background noise in addition to the music itself; Dolby systems help playback equipment decide which of what has been recorded should be played back and which should be suppressed. The development of organizational decision rules pertaining to information awareness is always problematic, given that such rules are always influenced by tradition or intuition (March & Simon, 1958). Cognitive limitations prohibit perfect rationality, leading to artificial simplification of the information about challenges which has been detected. According to March and Simon:

> The simplifications have a number of characteristic features: (1) optimizing is replaced by satisficing—the requirement that satisfactory levels of the criterion variables be attained. (2) Alternatives of action and consequences of action are discussed sequentially through search processes. (3) Repertories of action programs are developed by organizations and individuals, and these serve as the alternatives of choice in recurrent situations. (4) Each specific action program deals with a restricted range of consequences. (5) Each action program is capable of being executed in semi-independence of others—they are only loosely coupled together (p. 169.)

In short, organizations tend to pay attention to those things they have always paid attention to and in responding to those things, often do just what they have always done to get by. Organizations facing dramatic new challenges in their environments will, therefore, have trouble first in recognizing them and then in knowing how to deal with them. To adapt, these organizations must develop more sensitive detection devices and less restrictive decision rules regarding which information to pay attention to. Weick (1979) refers to the detection and filtering processes as "enactment," noting that the environment is often intangible and open to many different interpretations. Weick also notes that the process of studying the environment can change it, as when the price of a company's stock rises because a well-known investment firm is rumored to be studying its financial picture. In these ways, organizations often create their own relevant environments by deciding what they will pay attention to and what they will ignore:

> Investigators who study organizations often separate environments from organizations and argue that things happen between these distinct entities. . . . Having separated the "two" entities and given them independent existence, investigators have to make up elaborate speculations concerning the ways in which one entity becomes disclosed and known by the other. But the firm partitioning of the world into the environment and organization

excludes the possibility that people *Invent* rather than discover part of what they think they see. It certainly is the case that organizations bump into things and that their bruises testify to a certain tangibility in their environment, even if that tangibility can be punctuated in numerous ways. The enactment perspective doesn't deny that. But it also does not accept the idea that organizations are most usefully viewed as reactive sensors of those things that happen outside (Weick, 1979, p. 166, italics in original).

The importance of Weick's perspective for open sociotechnical systems design is that while the environment does present certain realistic constraints, it also presents opportunities. Managers and designers need to recognize constraints exist, and also challenge themselves to *create* the kinds of environments that best support their goals and values. By taking strong actions the environment can be transformed, not merely adapted to. Of course, deciding what actions to take can be as difficult as identifying the opportunities that exist.

Proposition 2:13. The greater the influence of tradition on decision making, the greater the expressed need to make "rational" versus creative decisions.

Proposition 2:14. The greater the perceived ability to influence the environment, the more innovative design decisions will be.

As noted in Figure 2-1, the process of selecting actions to be taken requires three more steps: (1) comparing the present situation to the past; (2) deciding whether new responses are required; and (3) developing the new response. As with enactment, selection has many pitfalls.

First, there may be no way of directly comparing the current situation with the past. How should automakers, for example, treat the entry of Korea and Yugoslavia into the U.S. market in comparison with previous entries by England, France, Italy, Germany, and Japan? Each of the preceding entries was different, making it difficult to know how to perceive these most recent ones.

Proposition 2:15. The more turbulent the environment, the more difficult it is to understand how current trends differ from past experience.

Second, it is extremely difficult for organizations to overcome habitual responses in order to decide that something new must be done. Existing organizational arrangements and reward systems typically benefit those who protect the status quo and punish those who call for change (March & Simon, 1958; Kerr, 1978).

Proposition 2:16. The more successful the organization has been, the less willing it will be to give up past behaviors.

Finally, it is difficult to invent effective response mechanisms simply because there is no experience to guide their development. Ashby's law of requisite variety (Ashby, 1960) states that for an organism to respond to a change in its environment, it must have within its repertoire of possible actions one that is appropriate to the situation at hand. If no such response exists, adaptation will not occur. The process of developing effective response strategies requires that organizational learning take place which is itself a process fraught with difficulties (Friedlander, 1983). To invent appropriate responses, organizations must do that which they were not designed to do. This requires breaking free of boundaries, roles and frameworks to experiment with new ways of doing business (Fry & Pasmore, 1983).

Proposition 2:17. The success of adaptation to environmental challenges is directly related to the availability of alternatives for action.

Once new behaviors are devised, there are still difficulties associated with introducing them to the organization. These difficulties become apparent in the last two steps outlined in Figure 2-1.

Introducing new behaviors in organizations has been the concern of organization development practitioners (French & Bell, 1973; Beckhard, 1969; Bennis, 1969; Huse, 1980; Beer, 1980). The process of sociotechnical systems change outlined in this book draws heavily on learnings from several decades of experience in the field of organization development, as well as modern ideas concerning the involvement of people in the design of their own work (Cummings & Morhman, 1987). Convincing people to alter their behaviors, whether through direct order or extensive involvement, remains perhaps the most difficult aspect of responding to environmental challenges.

Proposition 2:18. The more significant the adaptation to the environment required, the more difficult it will be to gain acceptance of new behaviors associated with the change.

Hopefully (and it is often only a hope), in enacting the environment, selecting strategies to adapt to it or change it, and creating new behavioral patterns among organizational members, some learning will occur. Certainly the performance of new behaviors requires learning on the part of organizational members. Beyond this rudimentary learning, however, the organization should learn something about both the environment and its own capabilities in adapting to it which can be retained for future reference. While memory can be a pest because it limits future adaptability (Weick, 1979), organizations with some remembrance of their past experience should be able to evolve more effective strategies over time as the results of earlier experiments become known.

Proposition 2:19. The greater the level of experimentation in organization design, the greater the likelihood that learning will occur and lead to more effective future adaptations to the environment.

The need for continued learning applies to the field of sociotechnical systems design as well. In data processing, for example, new technology is transforming the nature of work itself. In order to apply sociotechnical systems design methods to this type of work, entirely new analytic procedures have been suggested (Pava, 1983). Design recommendations, likewise, no longer reflect traditional sociotechnical systems conceptions (Taylor, 1986).

Building in opportunities for organizational designers to experiment with different designs that enhance their learning is difficult in the face of pressures to settle upon a workable solution that can deal with immediate environmental demands. Nevertheless, the inevitability of environmental change demands that experimentation with different designs will take place, either during the initial design process or later. To ignore opportunities for learning is to risk that the sensitivity of environmental detection devices will not improve; that blind spots in filtering mechanisms will prohibit important information from entering into awareness; that erroneous comparisons with past events will lead to continued complacency amid crises; that responses will continue to fall short of expectations and real needs; that new behaviors will be rejected; and that the organization will eventually be unable to acquire needed inputs from the environment.

The process of knowing the environment is a complex one and the challenges of learning how to transform it are great. Yet, regardless of whether the environment exists independently of the organization or is enacted by it, the environment imposes constraints and presents opportunities which influence the goals, processes, and outcomes of sociotechnical systems design. Because organizations depend on their environments for survival, no design can be considered satisfactory until it meets the criteria of environmental acceptance. At the same time, it must be recognized that environmental acceptance is transitory and that the ultimate objective of the design process should be to create the capacity within the organization for learning to occur so that continuous self-redesign can take place.

Techniques for Scanning the Environment

Given the impact of the objective and enacted environment on organizational success, it is clear that sociotechnical systems design must begin with an appreciation of organization-environment relationships. At a minimum, technology must be designed to produce products which the environment is willing to consume for the prices at which they are offered. Likewise, organizational members must be willing to work under the conditions created by the technical system if the technology is to be operated successfully. Inputs, in the forms of energy, raw materials, public support, capital, and other tangible and intangible assets must be forthcoming to maintain steady state operations. Beyond the conditions required to maintain the steady state, organizations are free to adapt to the environment as they see fit, or even create an environment more to their liking.

To understand the demands and opportunities the environment presents, organizational members must engage in the process outlined in Figure 2-1. As previously mentioned, two ways to begin this process with some rigor are open systems planning (Jayaram, 1976) and the search conference (Emery, 1982).

The open systems planning process involves the following steps:

1. List the important stakeholders in the environment and expectations they hold regarding both how the organization will operate and what it will achieve. (Note: Some stakeholders are both internal and external; employees are a powerful stakeholder group which at times functions within the organization but at other times functions as if outside of it.)
2. Create a realistic future scenario which depicts what would happen to the organization if no steps beyond those already planned or underway were taken to respond to stakeholder expectations.
3. Create an idealistic future scenario that depicts what could happen if either additional steps were taken to meet stakeholder demands or if actions were taken to transform those demands.
4. Compare the realistic and ideal future scenarios to identify design constraints and design opportunities.
5. Plan specific actions to support movement toward the idealistic future scenario.

It is important to note that open systems planning can be performed at any level of the system. That is, each group or level in the organization is capable of forecasting the expectations of stakeholders in its immediate context in order to develop an action plan for changes in its own operations. A production team might map out the expectations of other groups in the production system as well as top management, for example. In this way each unit of the organization is capable of involvement in adjusting to internal as well as external environmental changes.

The same is true of search conferences which take the following form:

1. The external social field (contextual environment) is explored; questions to be answered might include: "What broad social trends do we need to pay attention to?" "What new technological developments are occurring?" "What new legislation has been passed which might affect our future?" "What are our competitors up to?" "What values do people hold about their work?"

2. Broad desirable futures are then discussed: "What kind of work should people be asked to do?" "What would our organization like to be known for?" "Where are the greatest opportunities to improve?" "What impact should we have on the environment?"

3. The unique character of the system is then explored: "What is our culture?" "What is our identity?" "What don't we want to give up in order to change?"

4. Possibilities and constraints are explored: "What can be done?" "What can't be?" "What changes are realistic?" "What resources do we have available?" "How much time do we have?"

5. Operational planning is undertaken: "How will we make the changes happen?" "Who will take the responsibility for each action?" "How will we monitor our progress and evaluate our success?"

With either open systems planning or search conferences, choices of who will do the scanning and at what level of detail will influence the outcomes achieved. In some cases, top level groups do the scanning and then share results with others; in other instances, those who will actually work in the system being designed are invited to take part in the scanning process. Issues important to employees may not be as focal to executives and vice versa. Although greater involvement assures more complete depiction, complete involvement may be avoided because of time constraints or because the top level group wishes to maintain control over the broad design objectives that emerge from the scanning process. Often overlooked is the opportunity to involve important external stakeholders in the scanning process. Even though their presence may complicate the discussion, the information they provide is extremely valuable.

Detailed scanning takes longer, but produces a more complete depiction. If done with real commitment, the scan is capable of producing new insights regarding design possibilities. In a food processing plant, for example, a scan revealed that new product introductions had been handled in a way that produced growing alienation among workers. Since the scan also revealed that environmental turbulence was not likely to decrease, a new process for involving workers in product changes was devised. As employees began working with managers instead of against them, managers were able to concentrate more of their energy on dealing with external environmental challenges identified during the scan.

Proposition 2:20. The more involvement there is in the scanning process, the more commitment there will be to making changes in the organization to meet the challenges uncovered.

Proposition 2:21. The more energy is put into the scanning process, the more likely it is that attention will shift from exclusively internal to both internal and external opportunities for action.

Regardless of the technique used to scan the environment, the output of the process should include a vision of the organization and its future that can be communicated to all those involved in and affected by the design process. The quality of the vision statement is important, since it guides the energy and thinking of those who will contribute to the organization's success.

Proposition 2:22. The impact of a vision statement varies directly with: (1) the extent to which it is data-based and therefore convincing; (2) the extent to which it captures important sentiments of those it is intended to affect; (3) the extent to which it is viewed as realistically attainable; (4) the extent to which it is demonstrated to be of true concern to organizational leaders; and (5) the extent to which it is inspirational versus nondescript.

Implications for Sociotechnical Systems Design and Management

Figure 2-2 presents some implications of the open systems perspective for sociotechnical systems design and management.

In the next chapter we develop an understanding of the organizational social system and discuss its relevance to the sociotechnical systems design process.

There is no best way to organize. As the environment changes, so must sociotechnical arrangements.

The environment changes in both predictable and unpredictable ways. The challenge for managers is to anticipate the unexpected by building requisite variety, flexibility, slack resources, and learning capacities into their organizations.

Due to the significance of the environment, managers need to spend enough time on external issues to both manage organizational adaptation and create more desirable contexts for continued operations.

Each input-conversion-output cycle changes the nature of the organization's social and technical resources. Each cycle, therefore, presents an opportunity to either strive for joint optimization or move further away from it. Doing nothing guarantees that eventually the relation between social, technical, and environmental systems will get worse.

The environment is enacted, not merely perceived. This allows for limitless opportunities for change to occur. Success is possible through many different designs and strategies (equifinality).

Investments in environmental adaptation and transformation are as essential to success as investments in capital equipment and periodic maintenance. The more complex and turbulent the environment, the more essential these investments become.

Multiple sources of data concerning the environment are superior to single sources of data, particularly when those single sources are invested in maintaining the status quo. Wider involvement in scanning is superior to limited involvement. More detailed scanning is superior to less detailed scanning.

Environmental changes are the primary provocation and inspiration for organizational improvement. The more the organization is allowed to experience the effects of environmental changes, the greater the rate of improvement will be.

Figure 2-2 Implications of the Open Systems Perspective for
Sociotechnical Systems Design

CHAPTER THREE

The Social System

The social system of an organization is comprised of the people who work in the organization and all that is human about their presence. The social system encompasses individual attitudes and beliefs; the implicit psychological contracts between employees and employers; reactions to work arrangements, company policies, and design features; relationships between groups, among group members and between supervisors and subordinates; cultures, traditions, past experiences and values; human capacities for learning and growth as well as for sabotage and collusion; power and politics; individual personalities and group norms; the potential for motivation or alienation; for loyalty or dissension; for cooperation or conflict; and remarkable, uniquely human emotions such as love, hate, greed, charity, anger, joy, fear, pride, devotion, jealousy, compassion, and excitement. Organizations are, after all, no more than human creations and thus are fraught with issues arising from human limitations; yet they are blessed with the potential benefits of human intelligence and creativity. Social systems, while at times problematic, are the only parts of organizations that can conceive and implement improvements in organizational processes. Social systems are sources of adaptation, innovation, ideation, and inspiration; without them, organizations simply could not exist. Organizations exist to meet human needs; and no matter how sophisticated the technology they employ, organizations will always be subject to human influence. Thus, to design effective sociotechnical systems, we must define effectiveness in human as well as economic terms; and we must design organizations that tap the human resources that give life to collective endeavors.

More has been written about social systems since the early Hawthorne studies (Roethlisberger & Dickson, 1939) than any one reviewer could ever hope to capture or comprehend. The inherent emotionality, complexity and unpredictability of social systems has for decades attracted the interest of those who would aspire to understand them. Like some sub-atomic particle defying the efforts of scientists to prove its existence, social systems have proven to be fundamentally unfathomable. Like the sub-atomic particle, social systems are transformed by the tools observers adopt to view them. This keeps the question of whether the observer is seeing something that really exists or only the results of his or her own intervention open to continuous debate. Social systems are never at rest, but constantly undergo development, evolution, realignment, and transformation. Even if one could capture the true properties of a social system for an instant, the system would have changed by the time that the knowledge gained could be shared. These characteristics of social systems have made it exceedingly difficult to be prescriptive about optimal sociotechnical systems arrangements. Cherns and Wacker (1976) have stated:

> Anyone concerned with the study of organizations is entitled, if not doomed, to bewilderment when it comes to analyzing the organization as a social system. This is especially the case just where it ought not to be—in the work of the sociotechnical school where considerable attention has been given to developing methods of analyzing technical systems. The result is that we are able to specify in considerable detail the requirements of the technical system, but we have no adequate way of describing the social system let alone identifying its characteristics (p. 1).

The social system is the source of all adaptation to change, innovation, ideation, and motivation. Failure to adequately assess and design the organization according to the needs of the social system defeats that which is quintessential to the sociotechnical systems approach—jointly optimizing social and technical subsystems to create an organization which meets the demands of the environment as effectively as possible. While the ethereal nature of the social system makes precise joint optimization impossible, some aspects of social systems are more predictable than others, allowing joint optimization to be approximated. We discuss these aspects at the level of the individual, the group and the macrosystem. We then review analytical techniques and offer guidelines concerning the role of the social system in the analysis and design process.

Individuals in Organizations

Individual motivation is the engine that drives organizations to success. Too much motivation is seldom a problem; inadequate motivation often is. Sociotechnical system designers need to understand dynamics at the level of the individual organizational member in order to create systems which produce motivation, energy, and excitement in abundance.

The literature on motivation is broad and deep; a detailed review is beyond the scope of our work here. Instead some of the major contributions to the literature will be discussed in order to formulate propositions to guide our thinking about sociotechnical systems design.

The question of motivation appears to be a straightforward one. Maslow (1943) pointed out that only unfulfilled needs motivate behavior. Joint optimization, in this light, would seem to require no more than identifying which individual needs are not yet satisfied and then creating opportunities through work for their satisfaction. Indeed, much of our *Thinking* is guided by this very simple perspective; in *Practice*, however, identifying unfulfilled needs and creating opportunities for individuals to satisfy those needs through work is not easily done.

The basic step of need identification is complicated by the fact that individual needs vary, both among individuals and within the same individual over time. Therefore, no single design of work will maximize motivation of all organizational members or even any individual. Instead designs must be flexible, allowing individuals to specify needs that are important to them at any given moment and to permit the creation of structures that will facilitate the satisfaction of those needs.

Further complicating the process of need identification is the fact that we are often not completely aware of our needs; cognitive dissonance (Festinger, 1957), social pressure (Asch, 1952) and retrospective sense-making (Weick, 1979) are powerful forces which shape our desires, making it difficult to be certain whether our felt needs are truly our own. People often have difficulty explaining their behavior (Zajonc, 1980), let alone predicting how they will act in the future. Because of the difficulty people have in identifying their needs, we cannot rely strictly on their input to guide our design decisions. Instead we need to temper data we gather from organizational members with the results of our research and observations concerning what kinds of behaviors are likely to be triggered by various design features.

Proposition 3:1. The more the design of the organization permits the satisfaction of unfulfilled needs through work, the higher the level of motivation to work will be.

Proposition 3:2. Needs are neither static nor entirely understood. Therefore, the more flexible the organization design is, the more likely it is that continuous motivation can be achieved.

Proposition 3:3. Needs are often socially determined. Therefore, organizations which both create needs and satisfy them will be more successful than organizations which act only in response to stated needs.

For some time we have known that traditional organizational designs which emphasize bureaucratic procedures, narrowly defined jobs and tight supervision wreak havoc on the adult personality (Argyris, 1957). Normal adults have needs for learning and growth which cannot be easily met in traditional structures. At best, traditionally designed organizations are able to buy commitment to minimally acceptable performance by individuals in exchange for rewards which satisfy lower level needs (Galbraith, 1977). Excellent performance, in contrast, is closely related to the satisfaction of higher-order needs since it demands that individuals are committed to using their full capacities to solve problems, adapt to new circumstances and take advantage of new opportunities. Continued dedication to excellent performance is more likely to arise when needs for variety, learning, development, mastery, belonging, and generativity are met during task performance.

Proposition 3:4. To the extent that organizations are designed to meet lower-level needs exclusively, high performance is unlikely to occur.

Individuals are, by nature, idiosyncratic in their personalities and needs. Variability among individuals is of concern to managers of sociotechnical systems because it makes it impossible to design organizations which are universally motivating. Some organizations have attempted to limit the impact of individual variation on performance through elaborate selection procedures. Nevertheless, experience in these organizations reveals that variation will continue to pose design challenges as individuals test the limits of autonomy and flexibility out of self-interest. One partial solution to meeting idiosyncratic needs is to allow individual input to local design options. The issues and opportunities presented by self-design have been discussed by Cummings and Morhman (1987). Two outcomes typically associated with self-design are more flexible structures and enhanced understanding of reward systems. As individual needs are explored, clashes between different points of view result in reconceptualization of design options at higher levels of abstraction, freeing up possibilities for more individual influence over work arrangements. For example, in arguing over which of two benefit plans are superior, it may be discovered that there is no reason to offer a single plan; instead employees may be allowed to choose from several plans that best suits their needs.

Proposition 3:5. The greater the involvement of employees in the design process, the more flexible the resulting organizational design is likely to be.

Holding discussions about design also clarifies paths to rewards. The path-goal theory of leadership (House, 1973) suggests that leaders may improve employee performance by helping them to understand what kinds of behaviors lead to rewards of value. Self-design shifts the responsibility for creating this understanding from the leader alone to employees as well. Self-design may thus represent the most complete embodiment of participative management, as employees are involved in specifying both the outcomes they desire and the means they will use to attain them.

Proposition 3:6. The greater the involvement of employees in the design process, the clearer the understanding of how behaviors are linked to desired rewards.

No single sociotechnical systems design will match the needs of different organizational populations. Variations in life experiences, demographics, culture, values, skill levels, education, and perceived options for employment make each workforce unique. We know, for example, that there are differences in work ethics between rural and urban workers (Hulin & Blood, 1968) and cultural differences in attitudes toward authority. Optimizing the relationship between the social and technical systems of an organization requires a thorough understanding of that organization's population. Furthermore, to tap the population's commitment and energy over time requires continuous attention to the context of the environment in which the organization is operating.

Proposition 3:7. Designs created without the direct input of organizational members are unlikely to take into account the influence of unique population characteristics on reactions to design features.
Proposition 3:8. The greater the disparity between design features and the unique characteristics of organizational members, the less successful the design will be.

Thus, individuals provide the basic energy needed to make the organization run effectively; but they also, through their variability, make designing effective organizations difficult. These difficulties can be reduced by involving people directly in designing the systems they work and live in. Social systems are more than collections of individuals, however. In organizations, people are always involved in interactions with others; and interactions among people create group dynamics which influence the effectiveness of alternative organizational designs.

Groups in Organizations

Organizations are, by definition, collections of people. However, they are seldom random collections; observations of organizations reveal the existence of formal and informal social networks with enduring patterns of interaction among individuals. Groups, whether or not they are formed intentionally, are the basic building blocks of organizations. Groups are the vehicles through which most individuals develop a sense of identity and purpose at work (Thelen, 1954); thereafter, groups provide powerful rewards and punishments for selected behaviors on the part of their members which may affect task performance (Roethlisberger & Dickson, 1939; Asch, 1952). Groups are the setting in which basic interpersonal behaviors are learned (Bion, 1951) and are also the source of important judgments concerning values and status (Whyte, 1943).

Since members are attracted to groups for important personal and social psychological reasons, identification with a work group can be much stronger than identification with the organization. Given that groups often serve as the primary link between individuals and organizations, it makes sense to design organizations in ways that work with rather than against the powerful forces that groups exert on their members. In addition, designing organizations with groups in mind provides opportunities to take advantage of the superior creativity and problem solving capacity of groups in comparison with individuals.

Proposition 3:9. To the extent that the design of an organization is consistent with naturally occurring group processes, performance will increase.

Many factors influence the effectiveness of work groups. Prominent among these factors are the level of group cohesion, group norms concerning performance, and the stage of group development. Groups that are more cohesive have more control over the behavior of group members since members place greater value on the benefits derived from group membership (Sherif, 1936). There is no guarantee that cohesive groups will set high performance standards, however. Performance of such groups depends on whether members choose to support high performance or restrict output (Roethlisberger & Dickson, 1939). Group cohesiveness and performance in turn depend upon the level of group development (Bennis & Shepard, 1956); groups need to develop relationships among members and the capacity to regulate internal processes before cohesiveness and high performance are possible. Perfecting group processes which support excellence in performance therefore takes time and effort. It follows that when attention is given to perfecting group processes, organizational effectiveness should improve.

Proposition 3:10. The success of group-based designs for work varies directly with the amount of attention given to making group processes effective.

Likert (1961) described a number of factors which support highly effective group functioning. His observations are paraphrased in Figure 3-1.

Likert's list pertains to any kind of task group. Improving the effectiveness of work groups requires attention to some additional features of the context in which they exist. The following proposition is based upon experience with and observation of groups in sociotechnical systems:

Proposition 3:11. The effectiveness of groups in sociotechnical systems is related directly to: (1) the extent to which group members are technically proficient and, therefore, able to engage in technical problem solving; (2) the extent to which organizational reward systems promote cooperative behavior in the group; (3) the extent to which the group is provided with the training, support and resources required to accomplish its purposes; (4) the extent to which additions and departures to the group are well managed; and (5) the extent to which the group is able to manage its relationship with its environment.

Designing work for groups is not a panacea; when groups work well, the outcome of designing work for groups versus individuals can be better performance, greater commitment, higher satisfaction, greater creativity, better decisions, enhanced sharing of technical and nontechnical information, and improved flexibility. This is especially true when the work being done is highly interdependent, stressful, or insufficiently challenging if performed on an individual basis (Emery, 1963). People, however, do not always work well together in groups. Unlike in chemistry, mixing the same elements together under the same conditions does not always produce the same results where groups are concerned. Differences of opinion, value clashes, and struggles for status or influence can hamper group effectiveness. Figure 3-2 illustrates the

1. Members are skilled in the various leadership and membership roles required for effective interaction.

2. The group has existed long enough for good working relationships to develop.

3. Members are attracted to the group and loyal to its leader.

4. Members help to shape group values.

5. Members who link to other groups see a commonality of values across group settings.

6. Individuals support pivotal group norms.

7. Members are highly motivated to help the group succeed.

8. Members engage in critical but mutually supportive problem solving.

9. Leaders share information and create a supportive atmosphere.

10. The group provides relevant technical knowledge to help each member develop his or her full potential.

11. Group norms encourage striving for maximum performance.

12. Help is provided to members who need it.

13. Creative approaches are highly valued.

14. Value is placed on constructive but not excessive conformity.

15. Information is communicated efficiently.

16. Information is taken at face value.

17. Members share information crucial for success.

18. There is a high degree of shared influence.

19. Leaders are kept well informed.

20. The group examines proposed changes carefully, but is flexible when appropriate.

21. Individuals are free to make relevant decisions for the group.

22. Leaders are chosen carefully for their ability to facilitate the group's task and maintenance activities.

Figure 3-1 Likert's Properties and Performance Characteristics of Highly Effective Groups (Adapted from Likert (1961))

conditions most favorable and least favorable to designing work for groups.

As indicated in Figure 3-2, autonomous work group designs are best suited to situations in which there are no major barriers to sharing knowledge among all group members and tasks are routine. These circumstances are found in most manufacturing organizations utilizing technologies that are well understood. This kind of environment allows group members to acquire skills from one another and to gain mastery over task performance.

At the other extreme, tasks which are unstable and require the application of a wide range of highly specialized skills or knowledge are not usually conducive to group self-regulation. Temporary teams or task forces may be assembled to address a particular problem and then disband; medical operating teams are one example of this kind of situation. The stability necessary for group development is lacking here, as are opportunities for each member to learn the skills used by other members of the group. Under these conditions, self-regulation cannot occur effectively, since each group member has little influence over the others and little knowledge of the others' specialties. External control, either through direct supervision or deference to a coordinator (like the surgeon) is more effective here than self-regulation.

In the other two quadrants, conditions are moderately favorable for autonomous group activity. In the low specialization/low stability situation, group design will be effective if groups are able to shift their focus to new tasks without losing cohesiveness and a sense of direction.

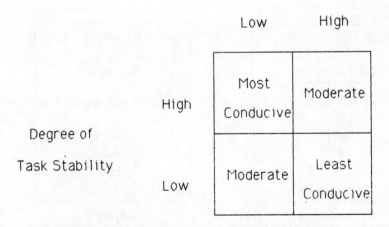

Figure 3-2 Most and Least Favorable Conditions for Designing Work for Groups

A city utility crew that goes from one type of routine assignment to another would be one example of this type of work design.

The high specialization/high stability environment, as typified by a commercial building team composed of an architect, engineer, construction specialist, financial analyst, and purchasing agent could also be amenable to group design providing that the differentiated knowledge of group members did not interfere with effective communication and task completion. Here the stability of the task allows group members to work together long enough to overcome the barriers to cooperation present in their initial work as a team.

> **Proposition 3:12.** The effectiveness of group designs varies directly with the extent to which: (1) the task of the group is stable; and (2) the knowledge differences among group members are small.

An additional factor affecting the success of group-based designs is the nature of the task assigned to the group. It is understood that at the individual level, holistic tasks which allow a person to complete a job from beginning to end are more satisfying than narrow, repetitive tasks (Hackman & Oldham, 1980). The same is true for groups (Emery, 1963). Groups are less cohesive when there is no apparent task-related reason for interaction among group members. A common task which provides a compelling superordinate goal increases cohesiveness and performance (Sherif, 1966). Kidder (1981) for example, has captured the stimulation which designing a new computer can provide for a group; whole tasks like this are more likely to result in group effectiveness than work which is not interdependent. Figure 3-3 illustrates two alternatives for forming groups in a metal parts fabrication process.

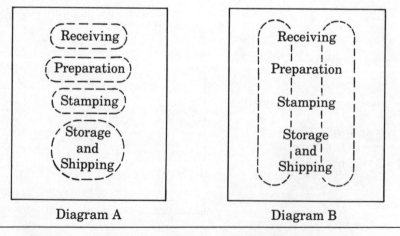

Diagram A   Diagram B

Figure 3-3   Options for Team Formation in a Metal Fabrication Plant
(dotted lines indicate team boundaries)

In the first class (Diagram A) groups are formed within discrete work areas corresponding to the major steps in the fabrication process. Although members are told that they belong to a team, their work is not interdependent. In the second case (Diagram B) groups are formed on the basis of completing the entire series of operations required to produce parts. If the design of work features job rotation, it is conceivable that over time each group member will work on each step of the fabrication process. In this case, the work of one individual is directly tied to the next; the group, therefore, has a task-related demand for continued interaction and problem solving.

Proposition 3:13. To the extent that group tasks are defined to encompass critical interdependencies in the work itself, group cohesiveness and performance will increase.

In summary, groups fulfill many important functions for individuals in organizations. They provide a sense of identity; help clarify values; set performance standards; provide feedback on status; stimulate creativity; enable problem solving; act as vehicle of change in the larger system; satisfy needs for belonging; provide comfort and support; assist learning; and enhance task performance. Despite these advantages, forming groups is not appropriate in all circumstances. Moreover, even when group formation is appropriate, there are many obstacles to effective group performance. Careful management of groups is required if they are to achieve their full potential. Groups, like individuals, are susceptible to pressures placed on them by their environments; for work groups, the most immediate environment is that created by the macro-level dynamics of the organizational social system.

Macro-Level Social System Dynamics

Two aspects of the larger social system which deserve special consideration in sociotechnical systems analysis and design are the culture of the organization and its structure. Each of these affects the way groups operate as well as the reactions individuals have to their work arrangments.

Organizational culture. Organizational culture has been defined in various ways. Schein (1985), for example, defines organizational culture as:

> . . . a pattern of basic assumption—invented, discovered or developed by a given group as it learns to cope with its problems of external adaptation and internal integration—that has worked well enough to be considered valid and, therefore, to be taught to new members as the correct way to perceive, think, and feel in relation to those problems (p. 9).

Kuhn (1974) defines cultural content as:

> ... artifacts, sociofacts (social structures and behavior patterns including rituals), language and its conceptual structure, performance skills, and the value attached to any of these (p. 156).

Kilmann, Saxton and Serpa (1985) refer to culture as:

> ... the shared philosophies, ideologies, values, assumptions, beliefs, expec-- tations, attitudes and norms that knit a community together. All of these interrelated psychological qualities reveal a group's agreement, implicit or explicit, on how to approach decisions and problems. . . . Culture is manifest in behavioral norms, hidden assumptions and human nature, each occurring at a different level of depth (p. 5).

Each of these definitions emphasizes that culture is the repository of knowledge and values that guide behavioral decisions related to performance. In essence, when employees are in doubt about what to do or how to feel, the organization's culture provides important cues to their sense-making process.

The importance of culture to sociotechnical systems thinking is twofold. First, it is important to recognize that all organizations possess cultures, whether or not they are apparent or well articulated. Therefore, outcomes of sociotechnical systems design are always affected by culture and, in turn, affect the culture, as design features bump up against basic beliefs, values, norms, expectations and ideologies. Thus, organizational culture can set constraints on what changes are acceptable. Second, design changes may influence culture in desirable or undesirable ways. Design features are more likely to affect the culture of new organizations than existing organizations since the culture in new organizations is only partially determined by the background and beliefs of individuals. In established organizations where the culture is more fully developed, achieving success in organizational redesign requires that the culture be assessed carefully to determine the fit between the culture and suggested changes.

Proposition 3:14. The stronger the culture of the organization, the more it will constrain design possibilities.

In the original sociotechnical systems studies of the British coal mining industry, Trist and his colleagues (Trist, et al., 1963) discovered that the traditional culture of mining conflicted with the changes introduced by mechanization. Traditionally, mining was performed in small, self-selected, highly interdependent groups; when new technology was introduced, so were organizational design changes that called for each person to perform a single task as part of a much larger team spread across three shifts and controlled by external supervision. The reactions of workers to the new arrangements were not favorable, leading to high absenteeism and low productivity. When workers were allowed to design their own organizations to work with the new technology, they duplicated their traditional cultural arrangements to the extent possible. Instead of single tasks, each person performed a number of different jobs as a member of a self-supervising work group. Productivity was higher and absenteeism lower in this culturally-consistent design.

This example suggests that it is important to assess an organization's culture before attempting to redesign sociotechnical systems arrangements. Once the culture is understood, the designer can either create arrangements that are consistent with the most important aspects of the traditional culture or work with organizational members to clarify why a change in culture is crucial and how such a change might be brought about.

In new organizations, efforts to deliberately create high performance cultures are becoming more common. The Richmond, Kentucky plant of the Sherwin-Williams Corporation is a case in point. An explicit philosophy (set of beliefs and implied norms and values) was adapted by top management and used as a reference in designing the sociotechnical system and in socializing employees to the work environment (Poza & Markus, 1980). Managers of the Richmond plant were not content to simply allow the culture to emerge; instead they wished to play an active role in shaping the culture in ways that would support their goals for plant performance.

Culture, of course, cannot be controlled completely. One reason is that culture is created in reference to the external environment as well as internal organizational conditions (Davis, 1985). Thus, the culture of an organization tends to become aligned with the influence of important constituencies outside the organization. Complex, highly differentiated environments tend to give rise to weak cultures, as different factions within the organization pay attention to the demands of various constituencies. Stable, undifferentiated environments, on the other hand, support the formation of strong cultures. Cultural barriers to sociotechnical systems change become especially apparent when an organization previously located in a stable environment enters an era of increasing environmental complexity. In such instances, the desire to maintain key elements of the traditional culture may interfere with efforts to introduce new design features which are better suited to the new context. Resistance to sociotechnical systems changes grows if the changes are perceived not as a way of preserving what is valued about the culture, but rather as a way of replacing the old culture with one more favorable to management.

As Deal (1985) points out, it is not too harsh to liken cultural change to a kind of death in the experience of employees:

People become attached to the elements of culture as the foundation of individual and collective meaning. When cultural elements change or are changed, people experience loss and react in much the same way as they would to the death of a spouse or to the loss of a home (p. 308).

Deal also notes:

On the positive side of organizational change lies some institutional patterns far superior to their predecessors in confronting the challenges of tomorrow and possibly even those of today. But lurking on the negative side of change is the reality of human suffering and turmoil and the possibility that natural reactions to uncertainty and loss may prevent us from ever moving far beyond ourselves. Unless we understand the process of cultural change and recognize that many of the changes we seek will result in the loss of existing cultural patterns and of individual or collective meaning, we may never fully attain the organizational forms necessary to meet modern challenges (p. 302).

Another aspect of the culture which is important to take into account during sociotechnical systems change is that multiple cultures frequently exist within the same organization (Louis, 1985; Davis, 1985). Thus, a design that meshes well with the figural elements of one culture may clash with those of another. Subcultures at the bottom of most organizations are quite different from those at the top. Davis describes the conflict between levels that can arise from differences in cultural beliefs:

Workers in non-managerial jobs frequently do not accept their unprivileged status willingly. An uneasy tension often exists between the managers and the managed. Those in non-managerial jobs find it difficult to accept the justice of a system in which managers have superior pay, prestige, and privilege as well as the power to tell them what to do. This produces a sense of resentment, which is heightened by the often monotonous, routine and dull nature of many lower-level jobs. Nonetheless, such a view is considered radical because it runs counter to the dominant culture—the managerial perspective—which is the prevailing way of thinking in organizations . . . . Organization members in lower level jobs are often united in a common distrust of management and in identification with actions and antics that can alleviate the boredom of excessively narrow jobs. In addition, organization members sometimes unite against other departments whose interests conflict with theirs or against customers, who are considered disruptive and unreasonable. A common formative element of culture at the lower organizational levels is the sharing of a common antagonism against the dominant managerial culture or against other subgroups internal to or external to the organization. This produces a sense of solidarity and provides a core set of values or beliefs that justify all sorts of behaviors and attitudes (pp. 165–166).

Davis notes that these cultural differences arise from two sources: (1) the role of concepts and symbolic interpretations of behavior (e.g., the way managers treat employees, or the use of the word "subordinate" instead of "associate"); and (2) cultural conflicts deriving from social values and social differences (e.g., societal views of the relative worth of executives versus lower level employees or educational differences). Thus, differences between subcultures require careful attention during sociotechnical systems analysis and the development of explicit design strategies to cope with the inherent conflicts they present.

In summary, culture is both an input and outcome of sociotechnical systems design. The following propositions capture some of the relevant points regarding the role of culture in high performing organizations.

Proposition 3:15. The more complex the external environment, the greater the potential for internal cultural diversity.

Proposition 3:16. The greater the cultural diversity within the organization, the more difficult it will be to achieve consensus on design parameters.

Proposition 3:17. The greater the cultural difference between management and labor, the less receptive employees will be to designs proposed by management.

Proposition 3:18. The better the fit between the organization's culture and its external environment, the more effective the organization will be.

The culture of an organization sets limits on what design features will be acceptable to organizational members and at the same time may be influenced by aspects of organizational design. Therefore, the design and culture of organizations are highly interdependent, just as are social and technical systems.

Organizational design. Organizational designs, like organizational cultures, are human creations. Designs are formalizations of social agreements that provide predictability and continuity, thereby allowing desired activities to continue independently of the individuals occupying various roles. Included in this definition are reporting relationships, rights of office, departmental boundaries, reward systems, policies, procedures, legal constraints, the size of organizational units, control systems, rules, information systems, and physical artifacts which help shape behavior.

Organizational designs are the tangible expressions of theories which organizational leaders hold about human behavior; the degree of formalization of control systems, for example, is representative of beliefs managers hold about the willingness, ability or trustworthiness of employees to make decisions that are in the best interests of the organization. Individuals take cues from the design to determine what management expects of them and what their relationship to management should be. Implicit psychological contracts (Barnard, 1938) are formed between employees and the organization as soon as roles and responsibilities are set out. These psychological contracts influence the level of commitment that will be put forth in exchange for the psychological as well as material rewards offered for task performance. Highly bureaucratized structures which spell out exactly what individuals can or cannot do send clear messages to employees that their judgment is not respected and their creativity is not desired. Flexible structures with little formalization send the opposite message.

In a recent article, Walton (1985) outlines two approaches to workforce management. The first emphasizes control while the second is calculated to produce commitment among employees. As indicated in Figure 3-4, the control-oriented strategy features jobs which are individually oriented and narrowly defined; performance measures which define minimally acceptable performance levels; a top-down, multi-layered control system; an emphasis on individual rewards; little commitment to continuing hourly employment; restricted employee input into decision making; and adversarial labor-management relations. Commitment strategies, on the other hand, produce organizational designs which feature the use of teams to perform whole tasks; an emphasis on innovation and excellent performance; flat hierarchies with widely dispersed decision making authority; group-oriented reward systems; a commitment to continued employment; widespread employee involvement; and cooperative labor-management relations.

Returning for a moment to the question of work group effectiveness in organizations, it is clear that commitment strategies which are expressed in the types of design features outlined in Figure 3-4 support successful group work. Walton and Hackman (1986) point out that high commitment designs produce the following kinds of impacts on group behavior: increased mutuality of interests between employees and employers; the development of norms that support high performance; increased capacity for self-management; improved managerial receptivity to employee inputs; enhanced status for group members based on task skills and expressed commitment; more equitable governance through the development of shared values; greater peer pressure; and more support for group work.

Thus, organizational structure is not inherently antithetical to sociotechnical systems design; but some structures produce results more in line with the objectives of sociotechnical systems design than others. The trouble with most organizational structures is that they are either too control-oriented or out of keeping with current sociotechnical/environmental arrangements. Most structures are created during the formation of the organization and changed only slightly thereafter. As a consequence, the need for control which was clear during the start-up phase is continually reinforced by the structure over time. Challenges to structural arrangements are difficult because of their historical success (Weick, 1979); so people at all organizational levels come to accept their roles as defined by the traditional structure rather than seeking alternatives. The alternative to an oppressive, control-oriented structure is not to abandon the structure altogether since too little structure can present as many serious problems as too much structure (Brown, 1983). Instead, the organization needs to adopt a temporary flexible structure, thereafter engaging in regular periodic examination of the structure to determine whether it is serving its intended purpose.

There is no single structural constellation that is innately right or wrong from a sociotechnical systems perspective. Instead, the fit of the structure with the desired social system dynamics is more important to consider. When the designer is interested in creating responsible autonomy at the lowest levels of the organization, decentralized structures are generally preferable to highly centralized ones; and when identification with a product or customer is important, product organization is superior to functional organization (Galbraith, 1977). When group initiative is sought, group rewards of some sort make sense; and when adaptability to a rapidly changing environment is demanded, it is usually best to minimize the number of rules which constrain behavior. In other words, every aspect of organizational structure can either support or detract from intended design outcomes; and achieving consistency in the signals sent to members of the organization through the design is as important as optimizing the relationship between social and technical systems.

Proposition 3:19. The effectiveness of group and individual activities in an organization is directly related to the extent to which the structure of the organization supports the performance of those activities.

Proposition 3:20. No single structural design will remain optimal over time; effectiveness is greater in the long run if a flexible structure is adopted.

Proposition 3:21. The most effective structure in a particular organization is one which fits with the realities of the environment and supports desired sociotechnical systems design objectives.

	Control	Transitional	Commitment
Job design principles	Individual attention limited to performing individual job.	Scope of individual responsibility extended to upgrading system performance via participative problem-solving groups in QWL, EI, and quality circle programs.	Individual responsibility extended to upgrading system performance.
	Job design deskills and fragments work and separates doing and thinking.	No change in traditional job design or accountability.	Job design enhances content of work, emphasizes whole task, and combines doing and thinking.
	Accountability focused on individual.		Frequent use of teams as basic accountable unit.
	Fixed job definition.		Flexible definition of duties contingent on changing conditions.
Performance expectations	Measured standards define minimum performance. Stability seen as desirable.		Emphasis placed on higher, "stretch objectives," which tend to be dynamic and oriented to the marketplace.
Management organization: structure, systems, and style	Structure tends to be layered, with top-down controls.	No basic changes in approaches to structure, control, or authority.	Flat organization structure with mutual influence systems.
	Coordination and control rely on rules and procedures.		Coordination and control based more on shared goals, values, and traditions.
	More emphasis on prerogatives and positional authority.		Management emphasis on problem solving and relevant information and expertise.
	Status symbols distributed to reinforce hierarchy.	A few visible symbols change.	Minimum status differentials to de-emphasize inherent hierarchy.

	Control	Transitional	Commitment
Compensation policies	Variable pay where feasible to provide individual incentive.	Typically no basic changes in compensation concepts.	Variable rewards to create equity and to reinforce group achievements: gain sharing, profit sharing.
	Individual pay geared to job evaluation.		Individual pay linked to skills and mastery.
	In downturn, cuts concentrated on hourly payroll.	Equality of sacrifice among employee groups.	Equality of sacrifice.
Employment assurances	Employees regarded as variable costs.	Assurances that participation will not result in loss of job.	Assurances that participation will not result in loss of job.
		Extra effort to avoid layoffs.	High commitment to avoid or assist in reemployment.
			Priority for training and retaining existing work force.
Employee voice policies	Employee input allowed on relatively narrow agenda. Attendant risks emphasized. Methods include open-door policy, attitude surveys, grievance procedures, and collective bargaining in some organizations.	Addition of limited, ad hoc consultation mechanisms. No change in corporate governance.	Employee participation encouraged on wide range of issues. Attendant benefits emphasized. New concepts of corporate governance.
	Business information distributed on strictly defined "need to know" basis.	Additional sharing of information.	Business data shared widely.
Labor-management relations	Adversarial labor relations; emphasis on interest conflict.	Thawing of adversarial attitudes; joint sponsorship of QWL or EI; emphasis on common fate.	Mutuality in labor relations; joint planning and problem solving on expanded agenda.
			Unions, management, and workers redefine their respective roles.

Figure 3-4 Characteristics of Control Versus Commitment Strategies (From Walton, 1985)

More will be said about the impact of different design features on behavior and effectiveness in Chapter 5 on sociotechnical design principles. Now we turn to techniques which can be used to assess the current and desired state of the social system.

Analytical Methods

There are many ways to analyze the social systems of organizations. All are inadequate to the task. The complexity and variability of social systems make attempts to fully understand them futile; even more futile are attempts to use the information that is gained through analysis to predict behavior of the social system in the future. This state of affairs is the source of endless debates among behavioral scientists representing different disciplines such as anthropology, political science, organizational behavior and psychology; each feels that its methodology for understanding social systems is superior to that of the others, while the casual observer wonders if ordinary people do not understand behavior better than the experts do. At this point, about the best we can do is attempt to capture the most essential characteristic of social systems in the hope that we might avoid organizational designs that either fly against existing traditions or fail to capture readily available energy. More precisely, the designer needs to know the answers to three questions: (1) What aspects of the social system do people wish to change or leave behind? (2) What aspects of the social system do people wish to retain or strengthen? and (3) What aspects of the social system should be created which do not currently exist?

The methods most commonly used to provide answers to these questions in conjunction with sociotechnical systems design are the GAIL method; role network analysis; open-ended interviews; and surveys. Each of these methods suffers from certain weaknesses; therefore, more comprehensive analyses will usually feature two or more of these techniques used in combination.

The GAIL method, popularized by the UCLA school (see, e.g., Taylor, 1978) is derived from Parsons' (1951) typology of social system functions. According to Parsons, every social system must solve four fundamental problems. These are: (1) Goal attainment; (2) Adaptation; (3) Integration; and (4) Latency or pattern maintenance. The GAIL method investigates how an organization deals with these four problems. Goal attainment refers to the need to set and achieve objectives that result in the ability of the organization to engage in resource transactions with its environment in order to ensure survival. Adaptation is the need to adjust the internal workings of the system to fit changing conditions or demands. Integration refers to the need to establish cooperative relationships among organizational members engaged in common tasks. Latency or pattern maintenance pertains to the need to socialize new members and to establish structures or cultures that provide continued stability. The GAIL method calls for the examination of various types of relationships within the organization (superior-subordinate, intergroup, interdepartmental) to determine how each functional problem is addressed, how participants feel about the current situation, and what participants would like to see done to address the functional problems in the future. In the GAIL method, as with some of the other social system analysis techniques, data are best gathered through a participative process involving people from all levels of an organization. Problems or challenges related to each of the functional areas are brainstormed, prioritized and selected for further analysis. In the adaptation area, for example, issues may arise in supervisory-subordinate relationships which pertain to the sharing of market and profitability data; employees may comment that adaptation would be more effective if they were allowed more complete access to information, which in turn would allow them to become more fully involved in the process of devising innovative, adaptive solutions to competitive challenges. There is no way to "objectify" or quantify the data that are collected using the GAIL method; instead, statements which are made often, with emotion, or with consensual agreement are usually given more attention during the design process.

Role network analysis is a schematic means of depicting the frequency of interaction among members of a social system. This type of analysis is useful in determining the interdependencies among individuals in the roles they currently occupy in the system. Role network analysis has the advantage of revealing how the organization *actually* works versus how it was intended to work; communication patterns evolve to simplify task accomplishment, and often fail to follow official channels. Key bottlenecks or resource persons stand out in network analysis, providing a clear picture to designers of areas for improvement or restructuring. One of the first role network analyses performed in conjunction with sociotechnical systems design was done by Rice (1958) in his classic studies of the Indian weaving industry. The diagram shown in Figure 3-5 illustrates that before the sociotechnical system intervention, the relationships among roles in the weaving process were exceedingly complex and needed to be coordinated by supervisors. After the sociotechnical systems intervention, the establishment of autonomous groups limited the number of relationships required to perform the task and therein reduced the reliance of the group on supervisory direction.

Attitude surveys, like the Job Diagnostic Survey (Hackman and Oldham, 1980), can be administered to large samples or complete organizations to obtain comparative data on reactions to work arrangements,

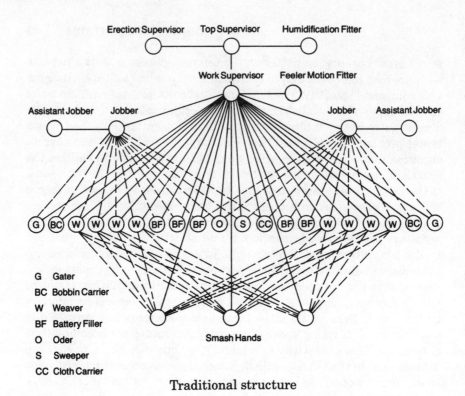

Erection Supervisor **Top Supervisor** **Humidification Fitter**

Work Supervisor **Feeler Motion Fitter**

Assistant Jobber **Jobber** **Jobber** **Assistant Jobber**

G BC W W W W BF BF BF O S CC BF BF W W W W BC G

G   Gater
BC Bobbin Carrier
W   Weaver
BF Battery Filler
O   Oder
S   Sweeper
CC Cloth Carrier

Smash Hands

Traditional structure

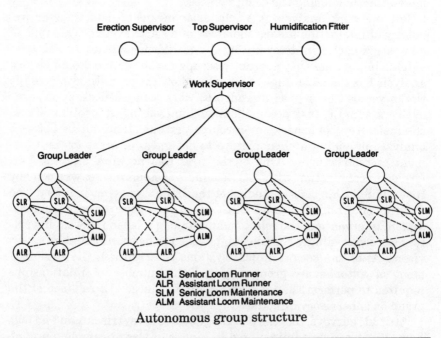

Erection Supervisor **Top Supervisor** **Humidification Fitter**

Work Supervisor

Group Leader **Group Leader** **Group Leader** **Group Leader**

SLR Senior Loom Runner
ALR Assistant Loom Runner
SLM Senior Loom Maintenance
ALM Assistant Loom Maintenance

Autonomous group structure

Figure 3-5 The effect of autonomous groups on role relations (From Rice, 1958)

46

job satisfaction, and individual needs. The Job Diagnostic Survey includes a measure of "higher order need strength" which is designed to gather data on the strength of desires by employees to satisfy higher order needs for learning, growth and self-actualization. Employees with strong higher-order needs are more likely to respond positively to the challenges presented by enriched jobs. The availability of normative data allows the comparison of Job Diagnostic Survey data gathered within an organization to a large national data base. The same is true of the Survey of Organizations (Taylor & Bowers, 1972) which was developed at the University of Michigan's Institute for Social Research and is designed to gather general attitudinal data.

Intensive open-ended or structured interviews may also be conducted to gain insights into more intangible aspects of organizational culture. Interviews allow the collection of idiosyncratic data which cannot be captured by standardized instruments. An understanding of the mining culture encountered by Trist and his colleagues (Trist, et al., 1963), for example, would not have been complete without insights into the rich history of the mining profession and the strong personal identities and relationships it produced.

The choice of questions used in diagnostic interviews is a matter of personal preference on the part of the researcher, tempered, of course, by indications of what seems important to know about in a particular setting. A comprehensive guide to diagnosis which will almost certainly uncover crucial data is provided by Levinson (1972). Some additional questions designed to get at relevant aspects of the culture of work organizations are presented in Figure 3-6.

Summary and Implications

When sociotechnical systems designers talk about optimizing the fit between social and technical systems, they are referring to an abstract, theoretical goal rather than a practical reality. The social system of most organizations is simply too complex and too rapidly evolving to be completely understood or controlled. Moreover, in any large organization, differences between social system dynamics at different levels or across different departments can be substantial; in actuality, there are many social systems in an organization, not just one. The challenge for sociotechnical systems designers is first to understand the constraints that social dynamics within an organization place on design possibilities; and second, to recognize that bold design changes can produce both desirable and undesirable effects on behavior.

The dimensions of the social system which are of concern to designers are correspondingly complex. At the level of the individual, important design inputs include the nature of motivation; skills and abilities; capacities for learning; adaptability to change; attitudes toward

1. What are the norms governing interactions among groups of people in this organization (supervisors-workers; union-management; co-workers; skilled trades-unskilled; women-men; black-white, etc.)?

2. How are disagreements among the same groups of people handled?

3. What stories are told to newcomers about the way things really are around here?

4. What does a new person need to know to do well here (new supervisors, new employees, new managers, etc.)?

5. Who are the favorite heroes or heroines among groups of people here? What stories are told about them?

6. What rituals or customs do you see repeated here?

7. If someone from another planet were to visit this organization, how would you describe to him or her what this organization does and how it does it?

8. What do you value most about working here? Least? If you had three wishes, what would you change?

9. What makes you committed to doing a good job? What gets in your way?

10. What is the most exciting thing that has happened to you since you have been here?

Figure 3-6 Some Suggested Interview Questions

participation; and historical experiences. At the group level, one needs to consider the degree of cohesiveness; the stage of group development; the quality of group processes; the nature of group norms; the nature of the group's task; the availability of resources; the effect of reward systems on cooperation; membership compatability and stability; and the level of group autonomy. At the macro-level, social system dynamics can be understood both in terms of the culture of the organization and its structure which includes the designation of departmental boundaries, reward systems, supervisory and control systems, job design principles, performance expectations, employee involvement opportunities, and the nature of contracts between labor and management as well as psychological contracts between the organization and its members.

In our increasingly complex and technological world, organizing physical effort has become less important to long run survival than tapping human creativity. The social system is the source of all innovation and adaptation. Because innovation and adaptation require human commitment, we need to understand how the design of organizations influences the willingness of people to help organizations succeed.

Organizational success depends on social system dynamics. Therefore, the social system should receive as much attention during sociotechnical systems design as the technology and the environment.

When it is possible to select members of a social system, as in a new organization or start-up of a new facility, the resulting culture will be stronger if members are relatively homogeneous in their backgrounds and attitudes toward work.

When selecting members of a social system is not possible, the design of the organization should take into account: (1) the things that people wish to change about the organization; (2) the things that people wish to maintain about the organization; and (3) the things that people wish to create in the organization.

Adult learning occurs primarily through experience; adaptability is a learned behavior. The more people are involved in experiences which allow them to influence the design of the organization, the more adaptable they and the organization will become.

Activities that offer opportunities to satisfy unfulfilled needs will produce more motivation than activities devoid of such opportunities. Whenever possible, it is best to create opportunities to satisfy higher order needs through the work itself and in ways that support organizational objectives.

High performance requires commitment; building commitment requires treating people like adults and engaging them fully in shaping their future.

Figure 3-7   Implications of the Social System for Sociotechnical Systems Design

Specifically we need to recognize that in the past, many organizations have been designed to control employee behavior and discourage innovation and flexibility. In sociotechnical systems design, it is recognized that the social system holds the key to long-run organizational survival and that its design should be a conscious, participative effort. Figure 3-7 presents some implications of the social system for management and sociotechnical systems design.

CHAPTER FOUR

The Technical System

Al, at the wheel, his face purposeful, his whole body listening to the car, his restless eyes jumping from the road to the instrument panel. Al was one with his engine, every nerve listening for weaknesses, for the thumps or squeals, hums and chatterings that indicate a change that may cause a breakdown. He had become the soul of the car.

John Steinbeck, *The Grapes of Wrath*

As this quote from Steinbeck illustrates, the relationships between people and the machines they operate often take on special characteristics. Although machines have no emotional capacity, we still imbue them with personalities in order to make our relationships with them more fulfilling. We imagine that machines possess human traits because we are social creatures, in need of emotional bonding; we imagine that machines care how we treat them and allow our own behaviors to be influenced by the physical properties, operational necessities, and performance idiosyncracies of technical systems. Over time, we begin to derive our identities from the work we do and the technologies we operate, so that eventually we find it difficult to imagine our lives otherwise; and when our technology wears out or changes, we feel a loss not unlike that which we feel upon the death of a close friend or even a family member. At a very fundamental level, it is our propensity to develop relationships with inanimate technological artifacts that explains why the interdependence between social and technical systems in organizations requires careful attention. The behavior of organizational social systems may not be *caused* by technical systems, at least not in the sense that technical systems think and act independently to produce certain behavioral patterns; but social systems, through their own complicity, are certainly affected by technical arrangements. Roles are created by virtue of technical demands; more status is attached to some roles than to others, and then powerful political forces are set in motion to maintain these status distinctions—and the technologies that support their existence. In a very real sense, organizational structures are created as the unintended consequence of technical systems design. The contribution made by Trist and his colleagues (Trist, et al., 1963) was to recognize that while the design of social systems often followed technical system mandates, the two systems were in fact separate—the social system could be designed intentionally to produce valued human outcomes while still meeting technological imperatives. Hence the title of their book, *Organizational Choice.*

In an era where technological advances are occurring much more rapidly than ever before, it is increasingly important to be thoughtful about the effects technology is having on social arrangements. Some, like the French sociologist Ellul (1964) are deeply concerned about the impact of our increasingly standardized culture on the future of mankind. Others, like Abernathy, Clark and Kantrow (1981) are more occupied with the impact technology is having on the competitive balance of power among nations. Here we are more interested in the way technology shapes the experiences of people at work and, in turn, how different work experiences influence organizational effectiveness. Against the backdrop of advancing automation, mechanization, and the dehumanization of work, sociotechnical systems design is a tempering force, balancing human concerns against the apparent juggernaut of increasing technological efficiency.

In this chapter we begin by outlining the forces behind the seemingly irreversible movement toward the replacement of human labor with technology. Then we explore the nature of technical systems and the relationship between technical systems and social systems. As in the previous chapters, we next offer some propositions concerning the design and operation of technical systems. Finally, we conclude with a discussion of techniques that have been developed to analyze technical systems, focusing especially on the method known as variance analysis, which provides rich input into the sociotechnical systems design process.

The Technical Imperative

Throughout history, mankind has sought to ease the burden of production through the invention of technological substitutes for human labor. More than any other species, we are gifted with the ability to analyze situations, determine what needs to be accomplished, and then create ingenious methods or tools for completing tasks in ways that minimize the time, effort, energy or attention required to achieve our objective. Our transportation systems allow us to move objects through the air, over land or across the water at speeds that are ten times greater than just 50 years ago. Our medical technology has enabled us to cure diseases, replace worn-out or malfunctioning body parts, and extend the average life span to beyond 70 years of age. Communication systems permit instantaneous dialogue to occur between any two points on the globe. Production technology allows the average person to afford goods once available only to members of the wealthiest class in society. And information systems, while still in their infancy, have already signalled their potential for extending what we can accomplish not just with our hands, but with our minds.

Some would argue that capitalism was the primary force feeding the industrial revolution (Mumford, 1934) but the industrial revolution has occurred in communist societies as well. Marx himself believed that transferring control over technology from the ruling class to the proletariat was an indispensable prerequisite to achieving his dream of a perfect society (Wheale, 1984). The drive towards ever increasing technological sophistication has been a consuming passion for many societies, transcending political ideologies and economic arrangements. The publication of Orwell's *1984* and Schumacher's *Small is Beautiful* gave some recognition to the drawbacks of blindly pursuing technological advancement; but society continues to follow what has been called the technological imperative (Trist, 1981). In this view, more technology and more efficient technology is valued over less technology, regardless of its impact on human systems. It is as if technology exists as a force of nature beyond human control, with its continuing development uninfluenceable by human desires. The clearest example of this is in the area of military technology, which no one particularly desires but which we seem helpless to do away with.

While it is recognized that the technology of production organizations has created unbearable working conditions for many and has increasingly altered or destroyed some of what was once held dear in terms of our social fabric, culture, and lifestyles, technology continues to advance in its own way. Progress seems to be defined as continued technological advancement, despite associated human costs. Human costs are often perceived as temporary and in any event, insufficient to outweigh the benefits to be gained from further technological developments (Noble, 1977). The force behind technological advancement is more ideological than economic; it is the belief that technology can eventually relieve mankind of the need to struggle for survival and, indeed, create the utopia that mankind is due (Segal, 1985):

The utopians were not blind to the problems technological advancement might cause, such as unemployment or boredom. They simply were confident that those problems were temporary and that advancing technology would solve mankind's major chronic problems, which they took to be material: scarcity, hunger, disease, war and so forth. They assumed that technology would solve other, more recent and more psychological problems as well: nervousness, rudeness, aggression, crowding and social disorder, in particular. The growth and expansion of technology would bring utopia; and utopia would be a completely technological society, one run by and, in a sense, for technology (Segal, 1985, p. 21).

The utopian view, to which most of us still ascribe to some degree, is a society in which work is replaced by leisure (or at least choice in how we spend our time), and all needs are served by a self-operating, self-sustaining technology free of the need for human intervention.

Confronted with the unexpected and unanticipated unraveling of their short-lived empire, Americans are now clinging to their epic myths of national identity and destiny, hoping for yet another revival. And central to these myths is a collective fantasy of technological transcendance. Whatever the question, technology has typically been the ever ready American answer, identified at once as the cause of the nation's problems and the surest solution to them (Noble, 1984, pp. vi-xii).

So, for the steelmaker faced with competition from low-cost Japanese imports or the automaker confronted with a recalcitrant labor union striking for higher wages in a time when profits have disappeared, the answer is the same—replace people with modern and more efficient technology. Eventually (and in a few parts of some highly automated factories, eventually is already here), the goal is to have factories that operate without labor—and without the damaging influence of human actions on operational efficiencies.

Unfortunately or fortunately, depending upon one's point of view, the utopian goal of an entire factory without workers is not likely to be accomplished anytime soon:

The notion of total machine control is false. As we have seen, engineers have not attained the necessary technical and mathematical understanding of complex production processes to develop comprehensive control systems—systems that can keep cost, volume, and quality at optimum levels. The production processes are hard to model, many relationships between crucial variables are only intuitively understood, and engineers cannot predict how extreme values of certain ambient conditions (such as the quality of raw materials) might change variables within the production process (Hirschhorn, 1984, p. 157).

Many examples of aborted technical replacements for human judgment exist; one recent example involved the production of utilities for an oil mining and processing firm. Since utilities production, including the generation of both electricity and steam, accounted for a major cost for the business as well as a critical reliability factor in operations, computer systems designers were set to work on developing an automatic system which would eliminate the need to depend on decisions made by those who currently controlled the utilities production process. The system, involving the complex relationship between energy inputs, conversion processes, and outputs, was difficult to model; consequently, after the system was developed and installed, it was rarely utilized. Management recognized after trial runs with the system that human operators, as limited as their mental capacities might appear to be relative to those of the computer, could still make decisions which were far superior to those of the strictly logical automatic system. The system is now used only when a trained operator isn't present to make decisions.

As this example illustrates, the promise of technology replacing labor and thereby reducing managerial dependence on emotional, imperfect human operators is often just a myth. In most organizations, people will continue to play key roles in core services or production processes. The goal, then, is not to create workerless factories—but instead to devise systems of people and technology that are as effective as possible. Indeed, if technological advancement has done anything, it has been to *increase* management's dependence on labor, since in many cases managers are no longer capable of understanding the technology that their subordinates are using to produce goods or provide essential services to clients. The organization of the future seems to be one in which fewer workers are present, but among those who remain, the demands for knowledge (and for better treatment) will be much greater. Under such circumstances, managers will need to utilize strategies that emphasize commitment instead of control (Walton, 1985). The sociotechnical systems approach to organizational design recognizes that human beings will continue to set limits on what can be accomplished technologically. It stands to reason that technological perfection, while it may never be achieved, can only be approached through the perfection of human systems as well.

The Nature of the Technical System

The technical system of an organization consists of the tools, techniques, devices, artifacts, methods, configurations, procedures and knowledge used by organizational members to acquire inputs, transform inputs into outputs and provide outputs or services to clients or customers. In the sociotechnical systems perspective, choices about such things as how the technology is laid out are as important as choices about which technologies to use, since the layout and type of technology both affect how humans feel about their work and consequently, how well they perform it. Likewise, in service industries, the procedures used to accomplish tasks are as much a part of the technology as the computers or typewriters scattered about an office. This definition of technology is much broader than one which limits consideration of technology to mechanical devices; it allows a more complete examination of how tasks are actually performed and how choices in sociotechnical arrangements have been made. At some point the traditional distinction between technology and organizational design becomes blurred; but we are less concerned with maintaining artificial distinctions than with understanding the ways in which work is performed and experienced.

Many classifications of technology have been proposed by scientists interested in exploring the relationship between technology and organizational characteristics. Woodward (1958) for example, divided manufacturing technical systems into three major categories: small batch and unit production; large batch and mass production; and process production. Her survey of 100 organizations indicated that the most effective firms utilizing each type of technology were structured in ways that matched their level of technological complexity. She concluded, therefore, that universal "principles of administration" were not as useful a guide to organizational designers as had been commonly believed. Instead, she advocated a contingency approach to organizational design which took into account the nature of the technology used to accomplish the organization's primary conversion process. While there have since been some questions raised regarding the generalizability of Woodward's findings, the validity of the contingency approach to organizational design continues to be accepted as more sensible than an approach which offers "one best way" to organize.

Thompson (1967) concerned himself with a broader range of technologies than Woodward, and so developed a classification of technology which included: (1) "long-linked"—technology which involved serial interdependence among sub-tasks, as in an assembly line; (2) "mediating"—technology which links clients or customers with service providers in standardized ways; and (3) "intensive"—technology which involves the use of a variety of specialized techniques to bring about changes in a specific object, such as the patient who is seen by various specialists in a hospital. Thompson argued that each type of technology required a different mode of coordinating the various interdependent performers who operated the technologies. Long-linked technologies involve sequential interdependence that is best managed by coordination through planning. Mediating technologies, in which one unit of the organization may interact directly with any other unit, are suited to coordination by standardization of practices. Finally, intensive technologies, which require reciprocal interdependence, call for direct mutual adjustment. Thus Thompson, like Woodward, argued in favor of different sociotechnical systems arrangements for different technologies.

Thus, while the relationship between technology and organizational arrangements is not strictly deterministic, choices made about technology do indeed influence choices made about other aspects of the organization. Whether conscious or unconscious, the choices made by those who design and select technical systems affect the way people in organizations behave and how well organizations perform. According to Davis and Taylor (1979):

> Starting with the position that psychosocial assumptions are part of technical systems design, the effects of technology are seen in light of a self-fulfilling prophecy. That is, the observed effects on workers and organizations of technology reflect the assumptions held by the designers of the technical system about men and social systems. Hypotheses held about the nature of man embedded within a technical system are operationalized in the technical system. For example, when assumptions are held that a system is composed of reliable technical elements and unreliable social elements, then, to provide total system reliability, the technical design will call for parts of people as replaceable machine elements to be regulated by the technical system or by a superstructure of personal control. On the other hand, if the system designer's assumptions are that the social elements are reliable, learning, self-organizing, and committed elements, then the technical system will require whole, unique people performing regulatory activities (p. 113).

The effects of technology on organizational behavior are apparent at a number of levels. Some effects are immediate and intended; others are more indirect and often unintended. All the effects are important to understand since it is not just what is intended, but the gestalt of the total system of both intended and unintended effects which gives character to the technical system and the reactions it subsequently produces (see Figure 4-1).

Following the convention outlined by both Rosseau (1979, 1983) and Hancock, Macy and Peterson (1983), the effects of technology on behavior can be investigated at three different levels of analysis: the individual, the subunit or department, and the organization. Beginning with the effects of technology on individual behavior, the most notable impacts are on individual productivity and work design. The primary

Level of Analysis	Direct and Indirect Effects
I. At the level of the individual	Work design Productivity Self-perceptions Psychological contracts
II. Functional unit or department	Role structures Physical layout Interaction patterns Supervisory behaviors
III. Organizational level	Relationships among departments Organizational structure Reward systems Organizational flexibility Overall competitiveness

Figure 4-1 The Effects of Technology on Organizational Behavior

function of technology is to enhance the amount of work an individual can accomplish and the reliability of individual performance. The nature of the technology (e.g., assembly line versus handicraft) sets limits on behaviors that are permissible in order for the technology to operate as intended and hence, determines the flavor of work experienced by individuals. Levels of variety, autonomy, feedback, task completeness, task significance, interdependence with others, and required skills are all affected, if not predetermined, by the nature of the technology in use.

Proposition 4.1. Generally speaking, the design of jobs will be more stimulating when the technology: (1) demands a variety of skills on the part of employees; (2) demands higher level skills which require time to learn and master; (3) requires higher levels of interaction among employees; (4) involves greater variability in inputs, conversion processes, and outputs; (5) is subject to continuous change or modification; (6) is designed to provide more direct and immediate feedback; (7) allows greater flexibility in geographic movement and in work patterns; and (8) leaves a significant degree of relevant decision making to employees.

Beyond the direct effects on productivity and work design, technical arrangements also impact individual behavior more indirectly. A person's identity and sense of self-worth are frequently related to the work they do; the surgeon and assembly line worker differ not only in the pay they receive, but also in their own appraisal of their ability to contribute to society in meaningful ways. The interplay between the roles defined by technology and one's self-image further gives rise to psychological contracts between the individual and organization which define the level of effort and commitment the individual will demonstrate in pursuing organizational goals (Barnard, 1938). Presumably, the willingness of physicians to work long hours, keep up with professional developments, and to place the welfare of patients ahead of their own needs is a reflection of their psychological contracts rather than formal organizational rules demanding such behaviors. In contrast, assembly line workers may shirk overtime requests, refuse to perform even small tasks outside of their formal job descriptions, and place their own welfare ahead of that of the organization since their psychological contract with the organization specifies that they should do no more than the absolute minimum required to earn their pay. It is not that assembly line workers are lazy or uncooperative; the nature of their work, as determined by the technology, creates extremely fractionated jobs that often require no more than a pair of hands; over time, as no more is demanded or even desired from people, supervisors and employees alike come to view the narrowly defined job as the maximum contribution to be expected. When more is demanded, the adversarial history of labor relations dictates that before more work will be done, a new wage must be agreed upon. For a person to do more work without demanding more pay would be a violation of both side's understanding of the legal and psychological contracts that guide proper behavior under these circumstances. Hence, the nature of the technical system used by an organization influences the apparent level of commitment and motivation demonstrated by individuals.

Contrary to the intentions of designers, over-simplifying jobs may actually lead to *Lower* productivity, *Poorer* quality and *Decreased* reliability of operations in the long run. Emery (1963), in setting out principles for work design, was careful to use the word "optimal" in referring to the degree of responsibility, variety and autonomy that should be accorded to workers, since either too little or too much of these job dimensions could lead to sub-optimal performance. Too much variety makes the job too difficult to learn and prevents the employee from developing a sense of mastery over it. Too little variety results in boredom, a lack of attention to detail and decreased motivation. Throughout much of the first three-quarters of this century, designers have erred on the side of extreme simplicity in work design, presumably to avoid difficulties in recruiting, training and replacing people. Simple job designs also meant utilizing an unskilled labor force, resulting in lower wage levels. The costs of this strategy are becoming painfully apparent as U.S. manufacturers struggle to keep abreast of their competition in world markets. For some organizations, changing the psychological contract between employees and the organization has proven to be difficult or impossible, making the introduction of innovative work designs infeasible.

At the level of the functional unit or department, technical arrangements affect role structures, physical layouts, interaction patterns and supervisory behaviors. Technologies which encourage skill differentiation among employees often cause boundaries to develop and become formalized through job descriptions and structural arrangements. Maintenance jobs may become separated from production jobs, for example; later, a maintenance department may be formed with its own supervisor; still later, the maintenance department may be physically relocated and the maintenance supervisor may be asked to report to the head of engineering rather than the production superintendent, making the boundary between production and maintenance even more formidable. Thus, specialized roles that develop in response to technical demands tend to restrict interaction patterns eventually and set limits on who should be involved in planning or problem-solving activities.

Boundaries created by technical arrangements are frequently associated with differences in the time at which different activities occur (first shift versus second shift); the territories in which work is performed (first floor versus second floor) or the nature of the technology being operated in different parts of the operation (stamping presses versus assembly lines); these boundaries are significant because they can interfere with interdependent problem solving concerning technical considerations (Miller, 1959). Difficulties created by these boundaries are called upon to compensate for the lack of spontaneous problem solving at lower levels in the organization. Supervisors may find their time divided between trying to motivate employees in jobs that are not designed to create motivation naturally and pleading for cooperation from their peers who manage departments with different interests and priorities. The styles supervisors use to carry out these functions are influenced by the psychological contracts between employees and the organization and by the organization's structure.

Proposition 4:2. Generally speaking, to the extent that the technical system creates barriers to cooperation either among peer groups or between supervisors and subordinates, supervisors will be forced to utilize more coercive or political styles to extract required behaviors from others.

Technological choices at the organizational level may influence relationships among different units or departments, organizational structures, reward systems, organizational flexibility and overall performance. Organizational effects are slower to develop and more indirect than those at the individual and sub-unit levels.

Relationships among units may be influenced by the nature of the technology used by each unit to accomplish its purpose or mission. In general, technologies related to the primary or core task of the organization will be accorded more importance, and their departments more influence, than technologies used to support the core task. Thus, in manufacturing organizations, production departments hold more sway than accounting; in hospitals, physicians have more influence than administrators. Since both support and core functions are critical to the success of the entire organization, support departments may resort to political means of influence when more formal means fail.

Organizational structure, which includes the design of the organization as well as formalized policies and procedures, is the direct result of political decisions concerning the distribution and use of resources. Since political actions are sometimes the result of technological differences among departments, technological choices may influence organizational structures. The introduction of new technologies, such as management information systems, may eventually result in changes in organizational structure which are intended to redistribute resources or authority over the use of resources. When several different technologies are utilized by an organization, a complex structure is likely to arise which reflects the political battles among supporters of each technology to gain control of decisions. Under such conditions, additional hierarchical levels may be needed to coordinate the departments associated with each technology (Lawrence & Lorsch, 1967; Galbraith, 1977).

As special skills are developed to operate the technical system, reward systems may become differentiated in order to recognize the differential contributions of various departments or individuals. Those who occupy positions that allow them to exercise specialized skills, control information or perform work more closely related to core versus peripheral tasks tend to be compensated more highly than those who do not. Differences in rewards reinforce the legitimacy of status, role and class systems and may interfere with collaborative problem solving. When an organization faces technical change, reward systems may impede the introduction of new tools that may also call for people to engage in new behaviors or otherwise upset the current status system. One can only surmise, for example, that decision making in the U.S. steel industry continued to be dominated by those who were most closely associated with the existing technology at a time when the environment was demanding that new technologies be considered.

As the steel industry example illustrates, organizational flexibility and overall performance can be hampered by technical arrangements. Technologies which prescribe narrow roles for individuals, produce psychological contracts which preclude learning or change, and are reinforced by structural arrangements which interfere with cooperative problem solving may result in total immobilization. Under such circumstances, changes of almost any kind are threatening, since they may undercut the personal or political security associated with traditional arrangements.

Proposition 4.3.   The ability to produce goods or provide services in a profitable fashion and in a way that responds to the demands of the external environment over time is in part a function of choices made about technology. Technological arrangements which minimize barriers to problem solving and maximize both cooperation and flexibility are more likely to result in organizational effectiveness over the long run.

Technical System Design Principles*

Given the potential negative influence technical arrangements can have on organizational performance, how should technical systems be designed? The following principles suggest some partial answers to this question.

1. *Variances should be controlled at their source.* Unexpected deviations from standard operating procedures, plans or normal routines, represent unanticipated or uncontrolled problems in conversion processes. Typically, these variances result from the inability on the part of employees to either: (a) identify the conditions which cause variances to occur; or (b) take actions to correct conditions that are likely to lead to variances occurring once such conditions are identified.

In the following diagram, a 10-step conversion process is portrayed in which the output from each step becomes the input to the next. In order for the final output to be perfect (variance-free), two conditions must exist. First, the original input to the system must conform to specifications. Second, each step of the process must be variance free, meaning that any variances which do occur in the process are identified and corrected before they can affect other steps. Any variance

---

* I am indebted to Al Fitz for his help in developing this list of technical system design principles.

which is created in Steps 1 through 10 and not corrected will be evident in the final product; an inspection function located at Step 10 may identify the fact that a variance has occurred, but the cause may not be readily discernable or easily corrected, since the system operates in an interdependent fashion. Small variances occurring in Steps 2 or 3 may go unnoticed, but develop major problems in Steps 7 or 8, resulting in the rejection of the product after Step 10. While final inspection processes may prevent the product from going to the consumer and in some cases may point to necessary rework to salvage the product, ex post facto inspection cannot recover the time and effort wasted in the previous steps. For maximum effectiveness, operators should be able to detect and correct variances *before* they result in further difficulties downstream.

In an actual example, a manufacturer of electronic devices utilized a complex production process involving approximately 30 steps and 200 people to make a particular product. After a period of successful operation, the percentage of rejects in the final inspection of the product grew dramatically. It took several months to trace the increase in rejects to new material used in the first welding process in the operation. Employees had complained about the new material, but their supervisors insisted on the change as a cost-saving measure. In this case, variances introduced during the first step of the operation made the work of hundreds of people in later steps fruitless. Employees had the ability to recognize the variance, but the system did not permit them the authority to correct it.

2. *Boundaries between units should be drawn to facilitate variance control.* When variance control within a single step or sub-operation of the conversion process is impossible due to interdependencies with other steps or operations, boundaries of the system should be drawn to include the interdependent units in the same department in order to facilitate the identification and correction of variances. For example, a sub-assembly which cannot be tested until it is installed in a final assembly should not be separated from the final assembly operation by physical or structural boundaries. Instead, the sub-assembly and final assembly operations should be combined to permit employees to work interdependently providing feedback and solving problems that arise. When merging two interdependent operations is impossible, efforts should be made to rotate members of the departments, create opportunities for direct interaction among members of the departments, or in other ways ensure that information flows freely and quickly across the boundary between the operations. In sum, it is easier to control variances when they occur within a single unit than when physical, technical, temporal, or structural boundaries must be crossed.

3. *Feedback systems should be as complex as the variances which need to be controlled.* This principle is a variation of Ashby's (1960) law of requisite variety, which states that a system can adapt to change only when it is capable of exhibiting a response which is appropriate to the new circumstances it is facing. In technical systems, variance control requires a system that is capable of detecting variances that may occur, even though infrequent or unanticipated. The trick, obviously, is to design an information system which is capable of anticipating the unanticipated so that employees may detect and respond to variances before they cause major disruptions in the system.

In many manufacturing plants, preventive maintenance is a substitute for appropriate variance recognition systems; rather than risk a failure, preventive maintenance is performed on equipment whether it is running well or not. Since there is waste involved in this practice, some manufacturers have begun to develop more complex systems that are capable of monitoring the state of equipment in real time—allowing them to perform required maintenance just prior to equipment malfunctioning and only when it is necessary.

As another example of this principle, in the wake of the Chernobyl nuclear incident, there have been increased concerns about developing control systems that will warn operators of potential problems in nuclear power plants, even when such problems theoretically should not occur. Without such systems for anticipating the unanticipated, variances can only be identified once their effects are evident—and in the case of a nuclear power plant, that's a bit too late.

4. *The impact of variances should be isolated in order to reduce the likelihood of total system failure.* Backup systems, inventories, modular equipment design and enhanced technical abilities on the part of employees are examples of steps that may be taken to isolate or minimize the effect of a variance in one part of the system on total system functioning. In the design of the Volvo Kalmar plant, each work team was provided with an area in which to store their finished sub-assemblies so that the team could stop its work for a short time to discuss problems without disrupting the activities of other teams. In a food processing plant, material transfer pipelines from one part of the operation to another were purposely lengthened to create an in-process buffer inventory, again to allow teams to meet to discuss variances without disrupting the work of other parts of the plant.

Although just-in-time inventory systems have several advantages, one disadvantage is that they make each part of the system more interdependent with others; thus, variances which occur only in one part of an operation may cause productive work to stop in the rest of the steps downstream.

Another way to isolate variances within subsystems is to make each step in the process more or less complete and independent of the others. Although the source of the following story is lost, it makes the advantage of combining discrete steps into complete subsystems clear. Imagine two watchmakers; each needs to assemble 100 parts to make a watch; the first does it by assembling all 100 parts and then beginning a new watch. The second does it by assembling ten sub-assemblies of ten parts each. In either case, the total assembly time for a completed watch is two hours. On the surface, it would appear that either technique would be equally successful; but if we add to this situation the fact that each watchmaker must stop work every 15 minutes to answer the phone in order to take orders for watches, the second method becomes far superior to the first. The first watchmaker, in stopping his work, must start over again because of the interdependence of each step in the process with the next. The second watchmaker loses only the time devoted to one sub-assembly; over the course of a week, the first watchmaker may find it impossible to produce even a single watch, while the second may have produced 20. In complex production systems which are highly interdependent, one variance may prevent the entire system from functioning effectively; but if the impact of variances can be isolated through technical system design, the system will function more effectively overall.

5. *Technical expertise should be directed to the variances with the greatest potential for systems disruption.* A Pareto analysis of most complex systems reveals that the majority of problems are caused by a relatively small percentage of variances. These variances, known as *Key* variances, trigger events which either by themselves or in combination with others, result in severe disturbances. Unfortunately, technical expertise is sometimes directed toward more trivial variances either because they occur first, more frequently, or are easy to solve. Solving the wrong problem quickly cannot make up for ignoring or failing to solve tough problems that have the greatest impact on overall effectiveness. In one glass-making operation, corporate management refused to allocate funds for studying the technical process in depth in order to develop more effective process controls. Tremendous inefficiencies existed due to the inability of operators to control the process; but since poor material was simply recycled and didn't show up as scrap, corporate management was reluctant to invest money in improving the process. Instead, the maintenance and engineering employees were directed to spend their time on routine maintenance and minor equipment repairs.

6. *Technological flexibility should match product variability.* Although single-product technologies are more efficient in high-volume, stable markets, the pace of environmental change is making the value of any single-product technology dubious. The continuing trend toward flexible technologies – capable of producing a variety of products – reflects the shorter life cycle for most goods. Expandable computers, multiple-test medical laboratory equipment, and computer-controlled metal-working tools are examples of the trend to make technology as flexible as the products which need to be produced.

While the need for more flexible technology is becoming more widely recognized, it is not as well recognized that flexible technologies require more flexible work forces. The move toward more flexible technology may require continuous learning and rapid adjustment on the part of employees. These new requirements of people may call for new agreements between labor and management regarding pay and work design. The organizational issues associated with the introduction of more flexible technologies are still being investigated (Davis & Associates, 1986).

7. *Technology should be appropriate to the task.* Because of the relatively large capital investments most technologies require, the tendency is to purchase excess capacity in order to avoid having to make additional (and frequently more expensive) investments to increase capacity as the market for the product or service grows. Excess capacity carries costs however, both in terms of capital being available for other purposes and inefficiencies of operation. Additionally, the tendency is to overproduce, hoping that the market will absorb excess production, thereby driving down the manufacturing cost per unit and justifying the investment in technical capacity.

To the extent possible, technical decisions should be market driven rather than being left to those infected with what Toffler has called "macrophilia" – the "bigger is better" syndrome. More preferable still is the modularization of the technical system, allowing enhancements in capacity and other features to be made only as the situation warrants.

8. *Inputs should be monitored as carefully as outputs.* The success of the conversion process depends on the quality of incoming resources – in this sense meaning more than raw materials; the quality of technology, employees, managers, and support systems all affect the outcomes of the conversion process. Organizations designed explicitly to achieve high performance typically pay a great deal of attention to whom they hire, where they obtain their raw materials, what kind of follow-up support is provided by equipment vendors, and how managers are trained. The optimistic belief that deficiencies in inputs can be overcome once they are inside the system needs to be replaced with a strong conviction that the best time to avoid conversion problems is before the conversion process begins.

9. *Core absorbs support.* In many organizations, efforts have been made to isolate core technical processes which add value to the product or service directly from support functions which are intended to increase the efficiency of the core functions or make it possible for the core functions to take place. The separation of core and support functions is often carried too far; bureaucratic barriers are created which interfere with the ability of the core operations to obtain the support they need when they need it. A separate quality control department may actually assume control of the production operation by shutting it down after a poor product is produced rather than working with production to identify and correct problems before they result in a poor product being made. A separate maintenance department may result in long delays before production supervisors are able to receive the attention they need to help resolve pressing technical problems. A separate materials handling department can result in operators waiting impatiently for material to be delivered to their work stations so that they can resume production. A separate customer service department can intercept feedback which might otherwise be directed to the people producing the product who could actually correct problems rather than just smoothing them over. By reuniting core and support functions, adjustments to variances can be carried out more expeditiously. In addition, the jobs created by combining core and support functions tend to be more complete, more varied, more demanding of skills and hence, more motivating. Given more complete control over the conversion process, employees are more likely to take responsibility for its effectiveness.

10. *The effectiveness of the whole is more important than the effectiveness of the parts.* Ackoff (1972) describes the folly of attempting to create the perfect automobile engine by identifying and assembling the best components from all engines currently in the market. The problem is that while each component might be the best available at its own function, it would not fit together with the rest of the parts—and even if it did, its performance would no longer be optimal, since it was designed for the specific engine it was taken from. An organization, like an engine, needs to be designed and operated as a holistic system. Improving the technology of the organization without improving human capabilities to operate the technology or the market's ability to absorb the increased output is tantamount to force-fitting a Corvette crankshaft into a Chevette engine and expecting it to produce more horsepower. Social, technical and environmental sub-systems are richly interconnected and organizational effectiveness depends more on their harmonious interrelationships than upon their individual optimization.

Creating high performing work systems using sociotechnical systems methods requires stepping back and looking at the interdependencies among the social, technical and environmental subsystems that make each organization unique. The technical analysis procedures which have become associated with the sociotechnical systems approach are designed to overcome the natural tendency to utilize a piecemeal approach to organizational improvement. The emphasis in sociotechnical systems analysis is more on the interdependencies among components or functions than on isolated problems.

Technical System Analysis

The primary objective of technical system analysis is to discover factors which, acting singularly or in concert with one another, detract from the effective operation of the technical system. These factors may be purely mechanical, as in the breakdown of equipment due to worn components; or human, as in the case of failures to inspect workmanship. Recently, with the shift in our economy from manufacturing to service, there has been some concern about the applicability of traditional technical system analysis techniques to non-routine, knowledge-based systems (Pasmore, Srivastva & Sherwood, 1978; Pava, 1983, 1986). Although traditional technical analysis techniques were never intended for application in non-manufacturing settings (Trist, personal communication), they have been employed there with some success (Taylor, 1986). In most service settings, technical system analysis is probably best accomplished using some combination of traditional and newer methods. Both will be discussed here.

Traditional variance analysis. Although the origins of the traditional approach to technical system analysis are not completely clear, one of the first major applications of the variance analysis technique was undertaken by Engelstad during the 1964-67 experiment at the Hunsfos paper mill in Norway (Engelstad, 1970). The process of technical analysis described here is an elaboration of Engelstad's approach and also draws on the analytical methods proposed by Emery and Trist about the same time (see Emery & Trist, 1978). The recommended steps in the technical system analysis process are outlined in Figure 4-2, and illustrated with examples from actual cases in the pages that follow.

1. Identifying key success criteria. In the Hunsfos experiment, success criteria included the amount of chemicals used to process the pulp, the yield of pulp per cubic meter of timber, and the cleanliness,

1. Identify key criteria which can be used to judge the success of the system.

2. Draw the layout of the system, noting the flow of material through the system and the physical/departmental boundaries that currently exist.

3. List the major steps in the conversion process in the order in which they occur.

4. Identify current unit operations which are groupings of steps in the process which represent relatively complete sub-tasks and which are separated from other operations by the time at which they occur, the place where they occur, or the technology used to accomplish them.

5. Collect data on variances which occur in each step of the conversion process.

6. Construct a variance matrix displaying interrelationships among variances within and across unit operations.

7. Identify key variances which are those that have the greatest impact on success criteria or that cause many other variances to occur.

8. Construct a key variance control table which indicates how key variances are currently identified and controlled.

9. Suggest technical changes to help prevent or control key variances.

10. Suggest social system changes to help prevent or control key variances.

Figure 4-2 Steps in the Technical Analysis for Linear Work Systems

tearing strength and brightness of the paper product. In a computer programming department, success criteria included user satisfaction ease of program maintenance, program development time, and program quality. In a research and development department, the criteria consisted of the time needed to develop new products, the ease of product manufacturing, and the reliability of the product once it entered service.

Generally speaking, success criteria are related directly to the organization's core process or reason for existence. In a few situations, it may be desirable to include other criteria as well. For example, in situations where safety is a primary concern, variances may pertain to actions that lead to unsafe working conditions and to those that pertain to core processes. The reason for identifying a limited number of success criteria is to simplify the analysis and help focus it on the most critical outcomes in a given situation.

2. **Drawing the layout of the system.** The primary purpose of drawing the layout of the system complete with material flows, work stations, and real or imagined boundaries is to assess the difficulties in

coordination posed by the design of the technical system or physical facilities. In an ideal system, no barriers would exist between highly interdependent operations. For various reasons, barriers often do exist—and often at the most critical junctures in the conversion process. Redesigning the layout or structure of the organization may be the only effective means of improving key variance control in some situations.

The layout of the Hunsfos mill is depicted in Figure 4-3. This figure demonstrates both the complexity of the technical system and the need for contact across technical boundaries.

In some cases, it is helpful to depict the network of interactions among workers to gain an appreciation of how variances are typically controlled. Referring back to Figure 3-5, (page 46) taken from Rice's (1958) experiment in an India textile mill, the network of relationships is depicted before and after the establishment of semi-autonomous work groups. The relative simplicity of role relationships among team members in Figure 3-5 helps to explain the greater success semi-autonomous groups had in operating the weaving technology.

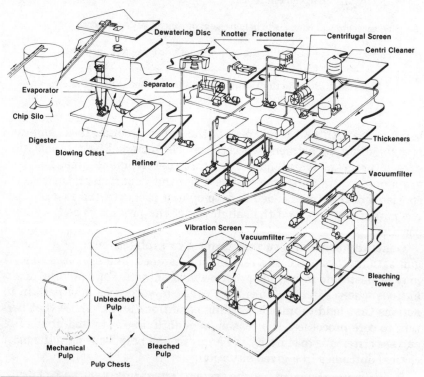

Figure 4-3 Layout of the Hunsfos Paper Mill (From Engelstad, 1970)

Again, from a design perspective, the layout and structure of the organization should complement natural interdependencies in the workflow rather than creating additional challenges to coordination. When interdependencies exist, the layout and structure should facilitate easy and direct communication so that those closest to the variances can identify and correct problems as quickly as possible.

3. List the steps in the process in order. In linear work flows, where the output of one step becomes the input to the next in a predictable way over time, the ordering of the steps in the conversion process should be straightforward. If the steps cannot be listed in order, either because they occur simultaneously or in an unpredictable sequence, non-traditional (non-linear) technical analysis should be undertaken.

Assuming for a moment that the process is linear, all steps should be listed in an order that produces an observable transformation in the product or the product's location. It is not necessary at this time to include preparatory or auxiliary steps which support the core process but do not result in direct transformation or relocation of the product (maintenance and quality control activities would be excluded here, for example).

Figure 4-4 lists the steps which needed to be performed in the coal mining operations which served as the basis for Trist et al.'s classic study (1963). The component activities (a-q) were for the most part sequential and predictable, making the work system a good target for traditional variance analysis (unfortunately, variance analysis methods did not exist at the time of Trist's study). The "main tasks" listed in Figure 4-4 could also be referred to as "unit operations," a term which will be discussed next.

4. Identify unit operations. These are groupings of conversion steps which together form a relatively complete piece of work and are bounded off from other steps in the technology by territorial, technological or temporal barriers. Furthermore, unit operations can be identified by their own distinctive inputs, conversion processes and outputs, so that each unit operation could conceivably be analyzed separately as an independent subsystem of the larger operation. The value of grouping tasks into unit operations lies in the fact that unit operation boundaries, whether they are physical or merely political, represent real barriers to interdependent variance control. Often boundaries which have been developed for managerial convenience or on the basis of geographical constraints are not aligned with natural interdependencies in the conversion process, making variance control more difficult than it needs to be.

In some cases, unit operation boundaries may be clearly defined on organizational charts. In other cases, some detective work may be re-

Main Task		Component Activities	Location of Activity
	(a)	*Turning and changing picks,* replacing worn picks on the cutter	Face
	(b)	*Jibbing in* the cutter	Face
Cutting	(c)	*Undercutting* the coal, timbering the face as cutter proceeds, setting nogs, scuffling	Face
	(d)	*Turning the cutter* at the end of its run	Face
	(e)	*Shotfiring* the undercut coal (by an official)	Face
	(f)	*Tracking through* the shot coal	Face
	(g)	*Breaking in* to the face	Face
Filling	(h)	*Filling off,* face timbering, clearing up spillage, and disposing of band	Face
	(i)	*Hewing* in the mothergate (also during cutting)	Mothergate
	(j)	*Coal drilling* commences during filling, continues with pulling and stonework	Face
	(k)	*Breaking and pulling* the belt conveyor and tension end	Face
	(l)	*Pulling up* the conveyor gearhead	Mothergate
Pulling	(m)	*Coupling up* the belt, replacing bars, tensioning the belt, setting the face signal	Face
	(n)	*Drawing off* the waste, resetting chocks and props	Face
	(o)	*Extending* the mothergate belt on alternate days	Mothergate
	(p)	*Stone drilling* (commences after [l]), placing extra supports, erecting forepoling, firing the shots (by the deputy)	Mother- and Tailgates
Stonework	(q)	*Pack building* in the gates and stowing in the goaf	Mother- and Tailgates

Figure 4-4 Steps in Longwall Coal Mining
(From Trist et al., 1963)

quired to locate them. Miller's (1959) paper on the differentiation of operating units in complex systems is a useful guide to searching for boundaries. Miller states that boundaries arise due to time, territory or technology. In Trist's coal mining case, for example, preparation of the coal face occurred on one shift, while removal occurred on another (time boundary). The problems that the preparers created for those who removed the coal were, therefore, extremely difficult to communicate about and control.

Territorial boundaries are evident in the auto industry, where plants producing sub-assembiles are located hundreds of miles apart or even in different countries than plants which assemble the parts into automobiles. It is not surprising that these territorial boundaries interfere with smooth communication and problem solving, or that each plant begins to care more about its own success than that of the whole system of plants.

Technological boundaries are created when departments are formed around similar technologies, despite the fact that there is relatively little interdependence among people operating the same kinds of machines when compared to the interdependence between sequential operations. In a light bulb assembly plant, for example, people who welded filaments together were located in one unit operation (easily identified because it had department status and its own supervisor), while those who attached the glass to the filament and socket were in another unit operation. The welders and final assemblers rarely interacted, despite the fact that they were more interdependent in determining the quality of light bulbs than welders were with one another. Technological differentiation is also apparent in Figure 4-4, where the "main tasks" were combined into unit operations on the basis of the type of work performed rather than the natural interdependencies in the coal mining operation.

5. Identify variances. Through discussions with supervisors, engineers and those who actually perform the work, variances are identified for each step in the conversion process. Since the number of variances can become large rather quickly (one research and development team identified over 800 variances which occurred in the process of introducing a new product), it is wise to focus on those that occur frequently or have the most significant impact on the system. Hypothetical variances—those which have never occurred but might—should be avoided unless their actual probability of occurrence is high or their potential effect devastating. In normal manufacturing operations, considering an earthquake as a potential variance would be nonsensical; but the effects of earthquakes are considered quite seriously in the design of nuclear power plants. Again, variances are defined as unex-

pected or unwanted deviations from standard operating conditions or specifications.

6. Construct a variance matrix. The most time-consuming and initially the most confusing aspect of variance analysis is the construction of the variance matrix. The purpose of the matrix is to display the interrelationships among variances in the conversion process. The matrix results in the identification of key variances, which are those that have the most significant effect on the operation of the system as judged by their impact on success criteria.

The first step in constructing the matrix is to list the variances in the conversion process in the order in which they occur, down one side and across the top of a sheet of graph paper. Unit operation boundaries can be penciled in between variances to help keep track of the operation in which variances are occurring and to denote barriers that must be overcome in order to engage in interdependent problem solving in those cases where a variance in one unit operation results in a variance occurring in another.

The working of the variance matrix involves reading down each column of the matrix (each column representing a single variance) in order to ascertain whether the variance in question causes other variances to occur. Like the mileage chart on a roadmap, each cell in the matrix represents the relationship between one variance and another. The absence of an entry in a cell indicates that the two variances in question are unrelated. When desired, instead of simply noting whether or not relationships between variances exist, the probability of severity of the problem caused by the relationship can be estimated using whatever rating scale one wishes. When ratings are done, the task of identifying key variances may be less difficult.

A simplified variance matrix for a computer software development process is shown in Figure 4-5.

In Figure 4-5 the unit operations are listed on the lefthand side of the matrix, encompassing a total of 16 variances. Three success criteria have been included at the bottom of the matrix for the purpose of evaluating the impact of each variance on organization effectiveness. Each variance is listed along the top of the matrix as well, so that each column represents the relationship between a variance and others that follow it (relationships are indicated with an "x"). At the bottom of each column, the cumulative impact of the variance on the success criteria is assessed using a scale that ranges from 1 to 3, with 3 representing a "very significant" impact.

7. Identify key variances. Once each variance has been evaluated in the matrix, judgments are made concerning which variances are most detrimental to performance. Judgments are based on: (1) the im-

Figure 4-5 A Simplified Variance Matrix for a Computer Software Development Department

Column headings (1–16) correspond to the same variances listed in the rows. Circled numbers (shown in parentheses) mark the diagonal; × marks indicate related variances. Success is rated on a 1 to 3 scale (3 = high impact).

Unit Operations	Variances	1	2	3	4	5	6	7	8	9	10	11	12	13	14	15	16
Program Contracting	1. Unclear user request	(1)															
	2. Unclear contract with user	×	(2)														
Program Planning	3. Inappropriate distribution of work	×	×	(3)													
	4. Misinterpretation of request	×	×	×	(4)												
	5. Unrealistic program plan				×	(5)											
Program Development	6. Inadequate skill	×	×	×	×		(6)										
	7. Mainframe use availability							(7)									
	8. Programmer turnover	×	×	×	×		×	×	(8)								
	9. Poor teamwork			×	×	×	×		×	(9)							
	10. Poor documentation								×	×	(10)						
	11. Poor test data						×		×	×	×	(11)					
Program Testing	12. Misinterpretation of results						×			×	×	×	(12)				
Program Review	13. Poor presentation						×							(13)			
	14. User changes request													×	(14)		
Program Release	15. Poor user education															(15)	
	16. Difficulties in maintenance																(16)
Success (1 to 3 scale; 3 = high impact)	1. User satisfaction	2	3	1	3	2	1	1	1	1	1	1	1	2	1	2	2
	2. Program development time	3	2	3	3	3	3	2	3	2	1	2	2	1	3	1	1
	3. Program quality	2	2	3	2	1	3	1	2	2	2	2	2	1	1	1	1

pact of the variance on the success criteria; and (2) the extent to which the variance causes other variances to occur. Variances are especially troublesome if they result in variances in other unit operations, since variance control is made more difficult by the boundaries between unit operations. Those variances which are judged to be most significant are categorized as "key variances" and in Figure 4-5 are denoted with a circle around their number in the matrix. There is no limit on the number of variances which are key; the idea is to select the most significant variances, since they will receive additional attention through further analysis and problem solving. In the technical system of the computer organization portrayed by the matrix in Figure 4-5, seven of 16 variances were selected for further analysis.

It is possible to use the variance matrix to display reciprocal variances (where a later step in the conversion process recycles into an earlier step) by making entries above the diagonal in the matrix. However, if a matrix becomes saturated (meaning that nearly every cell above and below the diagonal indicates a relationship between variances), the use of non-traditional analytical methods is in order.

Variance matrices become more sophisticated as technical systems become more complex. Figure 4-6, which displays the variance matrix developed by Engelstad (1970) for the Hunsfos paper mill, is more representative of what most finished matrices will look like. Here, Engelstad evaluates the significance of the interrelationships among variances and notes which variances are beyond control.

8. Construct key variance control table. The objective of this step in the technical analysis is to discover how key variances are currently controlled in the system. In almost every instance, the occurrence of key variances can be traced to either: (1) the inability of those who create variances to recognize that they are doing so; or (2) the inability of employees to take action to correct variances that are evident. Failure to control variances at their source can result in multiple variances downstream, which compounds the effect of the variance on the system.

The key variance control table, like the one displayed in Figure 4-7 for a food processing operation, indicates: (1) the unit operation in which the variance occurs; (2) the unit operation in which the variance is observed and who observes it; (3) in which unit operation the variance is controlled or otherwise corrected; (4) what control activities are currently undertaken; and (5) what information, technologies or special skills are needed to engage in control activities.

The key variance control table indicates clearly whether or not the person or persons who create variances in the system are capable of identifying and controlling them at their source. In every instance in

Matrix of Variance

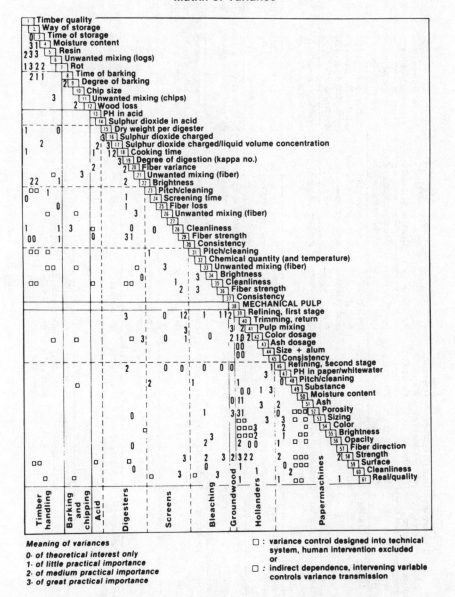

Figure 4-6 Variance matrix for the Hunsfos Paper Mill (From Engelstad, 1970)

Key Variances	Unit Operation Where Occurs	Unit Operation Where Observed (By Whom)	Unit Operation Where Controlled	By Whom	Control Activities	Control Information/ Technology/Skills	Hypothesis For Redesign
1. Ingredients unavailable	Preparation	Preparation (production operator)	Preparation	Inventory control	Check product levels/ production schedules	Economic order quantities/delivery/time	Preparation workers order ingredients
2. Storage time too long	Preparation	Preparation/packaging (quality control inspectors)	Preparation	Inventory control/ quality control	Check product life in inventory/run quality control inspections	Product life specifications/product quality test results/test equipment/ test procedures	Preparation workers perform quality tests
3. Preparation specifications inaccurate	Preparation	Processing/packaging (quality control inspectors)	Preparation/ packaging	Quality control	Product testing	Laboratory specifications/ results of tests/test equipment/test procedure	Preparation workers perform quality tests
4. Ingredient mixture incorrect	Processing	Packaging quality control inspectors)	Packaging	Quality control	Test quality; dispose of bad products	Results of tests on final products/test equipment/ procedures	Have processing workers perform tests
5. Mixer malfunction	Processing	Processing (production operator)	Packaging	Maintenance	Repair of equipment/periodic maintenance	Equipment specifications/ technical training/tools	Have processing operators perform maintenance
6. Product unavailable for packaging	Packaging	Packaging (production operator)	Preparation/ processing	Production planning/preparation production operators	Production scheduling/ processing of additional product	Sales orders; inventory levels/number of packaging lines in operation	Have meeting to coordinate production; buffer inventories
7. Product consistency	Packaging	Packaging (production operator)	Preparation/ processing	Production supervisor	Product inspection by quality control	Consistency standards/ process parameters/sampling procedures	Have preparation and processing workers check consistency
8. Machine adjustment	Packaging	Packaging (production operator)	Preparation/ packaging	Maintenance	Adjust machinery	Machine specifications/ technical expertise/tools	Rotate preparation/ packaging workers; workers adjust equipment
9. Storage time	Warehouse	Warehouse (inventory control)	Production scheduling/ outside of organization	Customers/production scheduler	Advertising, discounts/ adjust production schedule	Marketing studies/production capacities/product shelf life	Better coordination with marketing

Figure 4-7 Food Processing Key Variable Control Table

Figure 4-7, the persons creating variances were not responsible for identifying them; nor were they trained, equipped or authorized to correct the variances had they been able to identify them. One objective in sociotechnical systems design is to move the expertise that has been developed by specialists in variance control to the point at which the variance occurs. Preferably, skills in variance identification and control should be transferred to those who actually perform the work, since they are in the best position to spot variances and to do something about them immediately.

9. Suggest technical changes. The payoff in technical system analysis is the generation of social and technical redesign hypotheses to achieve more effective variance control. Technical changes may include improved information systems to enhance feedback to employees; the development of more effective process-control equipment; the evolution of more reliable or more easily repaired technologies; the development of more flexible technology; the reconfiguration of the technical system, workflow or workspace; improved inventory control or inventory handling systems; the design of more effective testing procedures; the building of buffer inventories for key materials or parts; the creation of more reliable back-up systems; or improved product distribution systems. Technical changes should work in concert with social system changes since the human system sets limits on the effectiveness of technical controls.

10. Suggest social system changes. Frequently the need to control variances can serve as the stimulus for redesigning work in ways that make it more challenging and meaningful. Since effective variance control typically requires learning new skills and taking on additional responsibilities, employees often welcome the opportunity to become more involved in making the technical process run more smoothly. In addition to training and subsequent job enrichment, social changes to improve variance control might include redrawing departmental boundaries, altering the roles of supervisors, changing reward systems, opening communication channels, initiating team-based work structures, rotating personnel among departments, initiating peer review processes, holding problem solving meetings, changing selection criteria, or reducing job specialization. Suggestions for changing the social system should be evaluated for their ability to contribute to improved variance control as well as against environmental demands, sociotechnical systems principles, and the stated vision of the organization's ideal future.

Non-Traditional Technical Analysis

In situations where conversion processes are essentially non-linear, such that the steps in the process cannot be listed in sequential order because they occur simultaneously or unpredictably, traditional variance analysis is of limited use. Special methods of thinking about and analyzing non-linear systems have therefore been developed (Pasmore, Srivastva & Sherwood, 1978; Pava, 1983).

Some of the features of non-linear systems which distinguish them from linear systems, in addition to the inherent difficulty in ordering steps in the conversion process, are that: (1) technology may not be physical but instead may consist entirely of specialized knowledge (as in some types of medical diagnosis); (2) the systems may have too few boundaries instead of too many (some managers of R&D operations claim that they never know what their employees are really up to); and (3) variances may manifest themselves in less obvious ways than in linear systems (the failure to communicate a crucial piece of gossip results in the loss of a big sale).

Since non-linear systems are often knowledge-based systems, it stands to reason that the level of knowledge availability and the effectiveness of knowledge application are directly related to organizational performance. Unlike in manufacturing systems, where knowledge is captured and made available in the form of physical technologies, knowledge-based systems depend on their members to create technology and apply it wisely. A hospital depends on its physicians to understand and apply medical knowledge; the effectiveness of the institution is directly related to how well physicians accomplish these tasks. Unfortunately for managers of knowledge-based systems, the exercise of one's knowledge is fundamentally a discretionary act; the manager can't reach into a person's head and extract the necessary knowledge or turn a valve to increase the rate of knowledge flow. Employees can choose to make their knowledge available to the organization or they can deny it. Hence, the quality of psychological contracts between employees and their organizations will have a tremendous effect on the performance of knowledge-based systems. This fact is reflected in the strength of the medical and legal professions, which seek to control the application of the specialized knowledge possessed by their members.

To control variances that might arise from whimsical decisions to withhold knowledge from the organization, efforts are sometimes made to formalize the psychological contracts between an organization and its members. However, the strength of such agreements is always limited by the ultimate power of the individual to withhold cooperation should the situation dictate. Because of the fear of jeopardizing relationships with key knowledge providers, non-linear systems tend to be underformalized and underbounded rather than overbounded (Brown, 1983).

Given that non-linear knowledge-based systems are subject to disruption by failure on the part of their employees to gather or apply knowledge, variances in non-linear systems are sometimes more difficult to pin down than in linear systems. Variances in non-linear systems may consist of a lack of knowledge, the absence of procedures to guarantee the effective application of knowledge, a lack of cooperation among interdependent performers or the failure of key actors to exercise discretion in performing their tasks. Likewise, controlling variances is made more difficult since constant negotiation is required to ensure the continued commitment of professionals to the success of the organization as conditions change.

Emery and Trist (1978) suggested an alternative technique for analyzing non-manufacturing systems which involved: (1) scanning the system to determine the overall purposes and layout of the system; (2) determining the specific objectives the system is designed to accomplish, including an analysis of all major outputs of the system in terms of who receives each output, what decisions it is intended to support, the contribution of the output to the decision, and the consequences of substandard performance on the social and economic success of the system; (3) analyzing how roles are designed to support the objectives; (4) identifying role interelations in order to discern what groupings of roles would be in order; (5) measuring each role against the psychological requirements of incumbents; (6) developing change proposals; and (7) instituting management by objectives techniques.

More recently, Pava (1983) developed a method for the analysis of non-linear technical systems which he labels "deliberation analysis." Deliberations may be formal meetings or informal discussions which shape the ways in which knowledge is applied to organizational tasks. The steps involved in non-linear analysis using the deliberation method are: (1) listing the key deliberations (those that have the greatest influence on how work is performed in the system); (2) assessing each party's contribution to the deliberation, including what each brings, what each wishes to take away, and the values or ideologies each holds; (3) identifying "gaps" in deliberations, which are missing parties, missing information or potential conflicts among discussants; (4) creating responsibility charts for deliberations which specify the proper roles for discussants during and after the deliberation; and (5) suggesting social or technical changes that could improve the effectiveness of deliberations. Generally speaking, the goal of such changes should be to bring the right actors together at the right time, with the right information, and with a willingness to work toward effective agreements which the parties are clearly committed to implement.

The deliberation analysis method can be used to analyze whole systems or discrete interactions concerning specific issues. As an example of the latter, Figure 4-8 provides an analysis of the parties to a deliberation involving the decision to undertake sociotechnical systems redesign in a unionized setting. This type of interaction is essentially non-linear; there is no predictability in the steps that will take place before the input (in this case an idea about improving the organization) is converted into an output (a plan that lays out how to proceed). The parties involved in this deliberation were the facilities manager, the employee relations manager, the president of the local union, and an external consultant. The gaps and associated variances in the deliberation are illustrated in Figure 4-9.

Party	What the Party Brings	What the Party Needs	Ideology/Values
Facility Manager	Knowledge of resources; corporate position; market forecasts; competitive situation	Sense of feasibility; knowledge of risk involved; sense of union commitment; specific steps to be undertaken	Concern with profits; minimizing disruption; satisfying corporate demands; need to innovate when possible
Employee Relations Manager	Knowledge of company policies; labor law; union contract; assessment of attitudes of labor force	Sense of union position on various issues related to proposed changes; sense of consultant's abilities to facilitate change without creating labor problems	Maintain cooperative relations with union; work toward increased flexibility for the organization; increase employee satisfaction
Union President	Knowledge of employee sentiments; knowledge of contract; recall of history of labor-management relations	Sense of benefit for workforce; information that will dictate the political position that should be taken.	Membership needs are foremost; job security and fairness of treatment are major concerns; maintaining delicate political balance between corporation and adversarial relationship
External Consultant	Knowledge of socio-technical systems theory and method	Sense of commitment by labor and management; sense of resources available to proceed	Humanism; developing a mutually beneficial relationship; making a significant change

Figure 4-8 Analysis of Parties to a Deliberation to Consider Sociotechnical Systems Redesign

Type of Gap/Variance	Description
Missing Information	−Accurate data regarding corporate support for STS −Accurate data regarding employee attitudes toward STS −Accurate data regarding middle management support of STS −Accurate data regarding the environment and necessity for redesign −Complete knowledge regarding long-term stability of key players −Knowledge of alternative approaches and their comparative success
Missing Parties	−Corporate representatives −Middle and first-line supervisors −Employees
Conflicts in Values or Ideologies	−Productivity versus job security −Stability versus innovation −Workforce flexibility versus protection of existing contract −Need for commitment versus desire to remain in judging mode as process unfolds
Lack of Cooperation	−Withholding information −Holding to a former political position
Failure to Exercise Discretion	−Unwillingness to take a position −Unwillingness to include others −Unwillingness to actively influence others −Resistance to experimentation or further learning
Lack of Procedures	−No agreed upon method of considering change other than collective bargaining

Figure 4-9   Gaps and Variances Associated with Deliberation to Consider Sociotechnical Systems Redesign

Figure 4-10 illustrates the value of responsibility charting; the actual process used for deciding whether or not to proceed with sociotechnical systems redesign involved only the parties identified in Figure 4-8; after the deliberation analysis, it was recognized that parties who possessed crucial information or would hold key positions during the implementation phase had been excluded from the deliberation. Moreover, it was recognized that the responsibility for the plan had to be shared jointly by labor and management. Social and technical changes in this instance involved informing all members of the organization about the proposed change, establishing new forums for communication between labor and management to discuss ideas or concerns, ac-

	Facility Manager	Employee Relations Manager	Union President	Consultant	Other Managers	Corporation	Employees	
Decision to Proceed	R	C	A	I	O	O	O	
Development of Plan	A	R	I	C	O	O	O	Actual

	Facility Manager	Employee Relations Manager	Union President	Consultant	Other Managers	Corporation	Employees	
Decision to Proceed	R	C	A	C	C	A	A	
Development of Plan	R	C	R	C	C	I	C	Ideal

C = Consult
A = Approve
I = Inform
R = Responsible
O = Not involved

Figure 4-10   Actual and Ideal Responsibility Charts for Deliberations to Proceed with/Plan Sociotechnical Systems Redesign

quiring additional knowledge of the process and outcomes in other organizations, and establishing a joint steering committee to oversee the change process.

As this example indicates, even organizations with linear core technologies occasionally encounter situations which involve non-linear conversion processes best analyzed using the deliberation technique. Given that this is the case, some combination of traditional and non-traditional methods of technical system analysis is usually appropriate.

Summary

The technical system of an organization determines the potential efficiency of its conversion process. But it also does much more. The technical system sets the stage for the evolution of social system dynamics and predetermines, at least to some extent, whether or not the organization will be capable of responding to changes in its external environment. Analyzing and designing the technical system of an organization for high performance involves identifying and controlling variances at their source, with the involvement of those who are closest to the work itself. Synergy between social and technical systems is achieved when organizational members are committed to operating technology in a variance-free mode and are supported in doing so by the organization and all relevant parties within it.

Once the technical, social and environmental analyses are completed, the challenge for the designer becomes using the information in a way that leads to consistent high performance. In the next chapter some features of innovative, high-performing systems are discussed.

CHAPTER FIVE

Objectives of Sociotechnical Systems Design

We do not yet know the potential productivity of our organizations. We judge productivity or effectiveness by historical standards, not by some percentage of the energy which theoretically could be directed toward organizational goals if our organizational designs were perfect. Currently, limits to productivity are both human and technical. No organization has developed its human resources completely; as far as we know, the potential for increasing human knowledge and creativity is limitless. Nor have we perfected technology; we are constantly amazed by advances in our technological capabilities, as machines evolve relentlessly toward greater flexibility and efficiency.

Two thousand years from now, the organizations of the twentieth century will appear as archaic, inhuman and wasteful of human and technical resources as the bureaucracy that built the Egyptian pyramids seems to us today. In the next century, we can expect to see changes in organizational forms that are as significant as the shifts in the last century have been. We aren't certain yet what these shifts will be; but we must recognize that while modern organizations are remarkably productive in comparison to their historical counterparts, they are far from perfect.

Many problems that stifle productivity can be heard in the laments of organizational members: "I wish my boss would get out of my way and let me do my job"; "This company doesn't give a damn about its employees"; "These people aren't motivated to work like we were in my generation"; "Those S.O.B.s in marketing really screwed up this time"; "How does headquarters expect us to meet our quotas with this lousy equipment?"; "I hate my job; it's boring, degrading, and dehumanizing"; "You can't trust anyone around here." The pleas for help go on and on.

Most, if not all, organizations use their human and technical resources inefficiently, as organizational arrangements interfere with potential performance. Knowledge and energy are blocked from application to important problems and opportunities; technology is operated carelessly and inefficiently; the wrong goals are pursued; inappropriate methods are used; cooperation is destroyed by interpersonal conflicts; people are improperly or inadequately trained and poorly matched to their positions; politics displace rationality; and the human spirit, which is ultimately responsible for all advancement, is trampled in the rush to maintain the status quo.

The very best of today's organizations will someday be regarded as wheezing and lethargic, just as we view the sweatshops of the industrial revolution today. Our best managers will be viewed as well-intentioned and even adventuresome for their time, but as ill-informed as the early pioneers of aviation. And finally, our society, built as it is upon the foundation of these organizations, will be thought of as backward and brutal just as we now consider those societies which exist without the benefit of electricity and modern medicine.

We are learning how to make organizations more effective. Sociotechnical systems design has not produced perfect organizations—but it is intended to create organizations superior to most in existence today. In this chapter, we elucidate the hidden assumptions behind the design of common organizations and then contrast these assumptions with the objectives of sociotechnical systems design. Following that, some features of sociotechnically designed organizations are discussed.

Shortcomings in the Design of Common Organizations

Common organizations (those not designed using sociotechnical systems concepts) typically suffer from a number of problems that interfere with their potential effectiveness. Not all organizations suffer from all of these problems, but most which derive their design assumptions from bureaucratic or military models display at least some of these characteristics. Although these models still guide most of our thinking about organizational design, they impose unfortunate restrictions on the vitality and potential success of organizations, as noted by Weick (1979):

> Whatever its origins, the military metaphor is a bad choice when it is used alone because it forces people to entertain a very limited set of solutions to solve any problem and a very limited set of ways to organize themselves. . . . Chronic usage of the military metaphor will lead people repeatedly to overlook a different kind of organization, one that values improvisation rather

than forecasting, dwells on opportunities rather than constraints, invents solutions rather than borrows them, devises new actions rather than defends past actions, values argument more highly than serenity, and encourages doubt and contradiction rather than belief. (p. 50).

Military/bureaucratic organizations, according to Argyris (1960) are at odds with the needs of mature adults. These needs include: being active versus passive; independent versus dependent; valuing new experiences and learning new behaviors versus performing routine behaviors; having deep interests versus shallow interests; having a long-time perspective versus a short-time perspective; valuing equality or superiority versus subordinancy; and being in control of oneself versus being unaware of one's own needs.

The military/bureaucratic organization clashes with these adult needs and thereby destroys productive motivation. The assumptions of military/bureaucratic organizational design include the following: people lack intelligence and therefore will perform most effectively when assigned to highly specialized repetitive tasks; there is one best way to perform any job; differences among people can safely be ignored; behavior can be controlled by transferring skill to machines and leaving no decisions for people to make; most people will be willing to forego ego satisfaction at work in order to earn enough money to satisfy their needs outside of work; people are primarily interested in making money, and therefore money is a consistent motivator; success or failure in an organization is a matter of how hard a person works; leaders should be more technically competent than their subordinates; leaders are fair-minded and unemotional; competition for advancement will sort out those best suited to lead; and all goals and decisions should be determined by superiors for their subordinates. These assumptions, according to Argyris, create an environment in which people are expected to behave more like children than adults: subordinates are to be passive, dependent, and respectful of authority figures; to hold a short time perspective; and to develop and value the use of a few shallow abilities. The result, Argyris notes, will be extreme frustration and psychological failure, leading to behaviors which are counterproductive to organizational effectiveness.

More broadly, Bennis (1966) notes that bureaucracies are susceptible to threats arising from rapid and unexpected change, difficulties in maintaining internal control with growth in size, problems with integrating the activities of diverse functions and complex technologies, and the dissatisfaction of their members. Instead, he argues for organizations which are more temporary, creative, and human-oriented.

Summarizing these ideas, it can be said that common organizations suffer from the following design ills.

1. *An over-specialization of most jobs.* Jobs are specialized in order to increase efficiency and maintain control over decisions; but beyond some optimal point and over time, individuals will begin to find jobs that are too highly specialized, boring, meaningless, and frustrating. The limits set by job classifications often interfere with the development of additional skills or the assumption of additional responsibilities. With time, both employees and supervisors come to view an employee's narrow contributions as the *maximum* that can be expected, rather than the minimum. When this occurs, the addition of responsibilities will be resisted unless more rewards are offered in exchange. Although extreme specialization has some obvious advantages in terms of minimizing training and replacement costs in the short run, in the long run these savings are often outweighed by costs associated with absenteeism, grievances, quality problems, labor unrest, lost productivity, and inflexibility in the face of change.

2. *An over-reliance on the ability of supervisors to control employee behavior.* The illusion of control created by task specialization is shattered when supervisors discover that they cannot control the complex interdependencies among individual task performers and as employees discover creative ways to beat the system. Attempts to regain or tighten control are often met with resistance, acts of retaliation, threats of unionization, turnover, or psychological withdrawal. The formal system declares that supervisors are more capable of making important decisions and solving crucial problems; but supervisors soon learn that their success will be limited unless they can count on the cooperation of their subordinates in providing them with timely information, ideas, and support. The effectiveness of a decision is discovered to be not just a function of the decision's quality, but also of whether or not it can be implemented. The informal system, which controls the success of decision implementation, can be more powerful than the formal authority system.

3. *Too great an investment in maintaining the status quo.* Once an organization has been designed, primary attention is turned toward the execution of current plans. Boundaries arise among functions as each attempts to accomplish its own objectives as it sees fit. Innovations are resisted because they threaten to upset work that is underway or the way things have always been done. Information concerning problems with the system is buried or ignored, and historical solutions are given preference as new challenges arise. Structural arrangements are perpetuated because people have come to value the security associated with them. Leaders, who have the formal power to change the design, find it difficult to do so, either because they don't wish to reverse their own decisions or because they find no favorable support from their subordinates. More often than not, efforts are redoubled to

make the existing arrangements work rather than to experiment with new designs.

4. *The breakdown of interdependent systems and activities.* Rather than recognizing the inherent interdependencies among parts of an overall process, activities are broken down into illogical pieces and further separated by physical, structural, or temporal barriers. At the microlevel, this shows up in the inability of a machine operator to assess the quality of the product he is producing or to make even minor adjustments to his equipment. Such tasks are reserved for specialists, who work in a separate department and maintain independent authority to perform their tasks. Although the operator is in the best position to control quality and ensure smooth equipment operation, distrust of the operator's abilities or motivation results in the creation of barriers to the completion of a whole piece of work. On a macro-scale, the breakdown of systems into components which interfere with the completion of overall tasks appears in the designation of departmental boundaries, the physical separation of interdependent technical processes or the allocation of particular activities to certain shifts. The belief that such separation has no associated costs forces the search for individual blame when problems occur, rather than a reexamination of the problems caused by the design of the system itself.

5. *An over-centralization of information and authority.* The belief that others cannot be trusted with sensitive business information or crucial decisions creates a self-fulfilling prophecy. When information isn't shared, people try to act on what information they have–with predictably poor results. The problems that are thus created reaffirm the supposition that people are incapable of acting intelligently or responsibly; decisions are then centralized even further and less information about them is shared. The more decision making becomes centralized, the less committed subordinates are to making decisions work. Information flow is further reduced in both directions, causing the centralized decisions to be made on even less accurate data. The poorer the centralized decisions become, the less respect subordinates have for superiors; sensing this, superiors lose more confidence and trust in subordinates ... and the cycle intensifies. Those at the top, with their greater legal rights, succeed in maintaining a false sense of control, but not without incurring costs in terms of decreased commitment and input into problem solving on the part of their subordinates.

6. *An over-reliance on individual monetary rewards.* Reward systems that are based on individual behavior frequently fall short of their desired impact for a number of reasons. First, they may be geared toward the wrong behaviors (Kerr, 1975). For example, organizations may desire high productivity but in fact be rewarding only attendance as high-performing and low-performing employees are treated the same.

Secondly, they may rely on monetary incentives long after small financial increases cease to be the most powerful motivators of performance. But most importantly, individual reward systems tend to produce self-oriented behavior in systems that are designed to function effectively only when people act in unselfish, cooperative ways. The idea that individuals should compete for advancement or greater rewards in the system produces competitive behaviors, political maneuvering, backstabbing, deliberate sabotage of others' work and the withholding of potentially crucial information. Because organizations are interdependent entities created to accomplish tasks that individuals could not accomplish by working alone, cooperation is essential to organizational effectiveness (Pasmore, Srivastva & Sherwood, 1978). But individual reward systems place self-protection and personal gain ahead of collaboration and thereby reduce the likelihood of successfully completing joint activities.

7. *The undervaluing of human resources.* The combination of bureaucratic depersonalization and an over-reliance on technical solutions to problems leads to the undervaluing of human resources. Human needs are regarded as unimportant and their satisfaction inappropriate in the organizational context. Instead of utilizing the flexibility and creativity humans offer, efforts are made to reduce or eliminate human influence. With the view that emotionality is inappropriate in the workplace comes the denial of the central role emotions play in connecting people to their work and to one another. With the belief that machines can be invented to solve every problem and to eventually replace human beings altogether comes disregard for human intelligence, adaptability and innovativeness. Human minds and emotions are essential components of progress and success over time; undervaluing human resources sets restrictive limits on an organization's future effectiveness.

8. *An over-reliance on technology as a solution to organizational problems.* Technology presents a most tempting weapon for combating organizational ills. Nevertheless, the belief that new technology will cut costs, improve decision making, increase quality or create impassable barriers to entry for others is often out of keeping with reality. Huge investments in new technologies may not result in the cost savings expected, particularly if the new technology proves too complex, unreliable, inflexible or costly to operate. Technology can create human problems as well if the working conditions it engenders are inhuman or unsafe. Common organizations fail to balance social and technical considerations, choosing instead to believe that once any technology is selected, it can be made to perform to its designers' expectations regardless of the situation into which it is introduced.

9. *Under-attention to the external environment.* Historical success, discomfort with change and personal investment by top decision makers in decisions that have already been made tend to limit the extent to which organizations scan their external environments (March & Simon, 1958). Because external environments pose the greatest challenges to continuity, organizations that either fail to perceive the changes that are occurring or resist acting on those that are clearly evident place their futures in jeopardy. The belief that organizational or technological perfection has already been achieved is difficult to overcome. Even when changes are considered, their cost is automatically presumed to be greater than their benefit. The burden lies on the innovator to convince others that his or her suggestions make sense, instead of the burden being on the protectors of the status quo to demonstrate why they shouldn't change. The external environment is the ultimate authority in determining organizational survival; but most common organizations are designed to prevent all but a few people from being concerned about understanding its demands and formulating strategies to respond to them.

Sociotechnical systems thinking developed as an antidote to the ills of military/bureaucratic organizational designs. Lower-than-expected productivity, poor quality, high levels of alienation and the inability to introduce innovations were clear signs that traditional designs were not working as well as they were supposed to. Moreover, it was recognized that even the most advanced technical systems required human direction, maintenance and improvement. This made the goal of designing human variation out of organizations unattractive. Instead, the search for alternative organizational design assumptions began – with the result that today, we can point clearly to the intended advantages of sociotechnical systems design over traditional arrangements.

Features of Sociotechnically Designed Organizations

Principles for the design of organizations using sociotechnical system concepts have been put forth by Emery (1963) and Cherns (1976), among others. Included in the lists of admonitions to designers are urgings to create optimal variety in tasks; to construct meaningful patterns of tasks that lead to holistic jobs; to optimize the length of the work cycle; to leave scope for workers to set their own standards and determine their own means of production; to include auxiliary tasks such as maintenance and quality control in primary jobs; to ensure that jobs are worthy of respect in the community and contribute directly to the end product; to employ various forms of group work when tasks are interdependent; to ensure worker involvement in the design of tasks; to allow workers to select their peers and supervisors; to make certain that the design of the organization fits with the goals intended and that each part of the design fits with the others; to control technical variances at their source; to create jobs that require multiple skills; to locate boundaries among departments appropriately; to ensure that information is available to all who need it to make sound and timely decisions; to provide opportunities for individuals to meet needs for growth, learning, decision making, social support and recognition; and to put in place processes that encourage reexamination of the design itself.

In this section, we consider the main advantages of sociotechnical systems design over common organizational design and use examples from actual organizations to illustrate how the design principles have been applied. To make the comparison and discussion more simple, the advantages of sociotechnical systems design have been grouped into six categories: (1) innovation versus preserving the status quo; (2) development of human resources; (3) awareness of the external environment; (4) maximizing cooperative effort; (5) developing commitment and energy; and (6) utilizing social and technical resources effectively.

1. *Innovation versus preserving the status quo.* Innovation, as defined here, is the creative employment of organizational resources for the purpose of enhancing organizational design, products, services, policies, work design or technology. Organizations which becom more nimble by enhancing their capacity to innovate should achieve superior performance both by attaining a better fit with their environment and by utilizing their resources more effectively than their traditional counterparts. Of course, too rapid a rate of innovation can tax an organization's capacity to support and sustain change. Likewise, the disorganization which accompanies change will consume more resources than maintaining the steady state. Still, the more innovative organization will have more and better opportunities for improvement and will also find it easier to implement changes that are selected.

In traditional organizations, management by measurement and control is used to force behavior into the mold created by existing plans and structural arrangements. This type of management is based upon the assumptions that existing plans are perfect, or at least superior; that switching directions would entail greater risks; that people do not have the capacity to contribute to improvements in existing arrangements; and that management will be able to respond to any problems that arise when the need becomes evident. Employees in traditional organizations are punished for their mistakes; differences of opinion are regarded as signs of unhealthy conflict; little attention is devoted to learning; and changes of almost any kind are likely to be resisted.

To enhance innovation, sociotechnical systems design calls for organizations to become more receptive to new ideas, more flexible in their designs, more participative in their management, and more promotive of learning and risk taking. In Data General and Apple Computers, receptivity to new ideas is demonstrated through the authorization of innovation teams; at 3M, intrapreneurs are entrusted with substantial resources and autonomy once their ideas are developed through less formal channels; other organizations, like General Electric, have been known to offer sizeable rewards to employees for good suggestions.

In Goodyear and Dana, flexible organization designs allow resources to be shifted to where they are needed most, with a minimum of policies to hinder adaptability. At some DEC and Sherwin Williams plants, participative management encourages employees to become more involved in problem solving, from which they learn more about the organization and are able to spot even more opportunities for improvement. Innovation also requires an investment in education for employees, often beyond the minimum required for successful task performance. Harmon Industries was a leader in offering employees opportunities for education in job-related as well as nonjob-related areas at company expense.

Risk taking must be encouraged by celebrating both successes and failed attempts (Peters & Waterman, 1982). Indeed, innovation requires re-learning *how* to learn, by focusing on the demands of the future rather than becoming trapped within the knowledge of the past (Schon, 1971). As a part of learning, differences of opinion will arise naturally; rather than quelling such differences, innovative organizations encourage the expression and understanding of countervailing points of view (Brown, 1983; Friedlander, 1983).

Finally, sociotechnical systems design encourages viewing change as healthy rather than something to be avoided. The establishment of permanent cross-sectional teams to consider ongoing organizational change is one way to ensure that innovation will become an ongoing part of organizational life (Stein & Kanter, 1980).

We are just beginning to understand how innovation occurs in organizations. Sociotechnical systems designs of the future will take advantage of what we are currently learning to create organizations that are more agile in their environments, more adaptable to human needs and more flexible in their development and utilization of technology.

2. *Development of human resources.* Critics of some "greenfield" experiments like the Gaines pet food plant in Topeka, Kansas or Zilog's Nampa, Idaho facility argue that the phenomenal results achieved were due to the fact that these organizations were extremely selective in choosing their labor forces. While no doubt true in part, the argument

is both insufficient to explain the outcomes observed and inadequate to excuse existing facilities from experimenting with sociotechnical systems design. The implication of the argument is that employees in existing operations are incapable of developing abilities that could rival the talents of employees in showcase operations; but few organizations have put this assumption to the test.

Experimentation in educational environments tells us that adults are capable of tremendous growth and learning (Livingston, 1969; Eden, 1988). There is no reason to suppose that these findings should not apply to the organizational setting as well. While the research in organizations is sparse, what there is is encouraging (Pasmore & King, 1978; Trist, Brown & Susman, 1977; Taylor, 1977).

From a theoretical standpoint, the effectiveness of an organization will always be sub-optimal as long as its human resources are less than fully developed. It would not be an exaggeration to state that sociotechnical systems designs will work only as well as the capabilities of employees allow them to. In at least two instances, failure to provide employees with proper training has led to the abandoning of sociotechnical systems working arrangements (Cummings & Srivastva, 1977; Tichy & Nisberg, 1976).

Sociotechnical systems design encourages employees to develop their knowledge in a number of ways. Some organizations (Gaines-Topeka, DEC-Enfield, Sherwin Williams-Richmond, GE-Bromont, Goodyear-Asheboro) reward employees according to the number of skills they are capable of performing. In most of these organizations, there are no limits placed on the number of employees who can eventually earn the top pay rate, which may require knowing how to perform virtually every job in the plant.

The development of abilities is also encouraged by the creation of jobs which demand multiple skills. In the same organizations just mentioned, employees typically perform a combination of production, maintenance, quality control, and managerial activities. Clearly, training employees for these jobs requires an unusual commitment to education by these organizations. Some of the organizations utilize peers as on-the-job trainers; others make arrangements with local vocational schools or colleges to provide optional training after hours. Typically, the expense of such training is borne by the organization; employees may or may not be paid for the time they spend at school. To reinforce the training, some organizations pay higher rates for learning skills only when employees are actually performing tasks which require those skills. Other organizations, like GM's Fitzgerald, Georgia plant, have regular requirements for job rotation.

In all of these cases, expansion of responsibilities accompanies the acquisition of higher level skills. Sociotechnical systems design does not endorse horizontal job enlargement, in which several jobs requiring the same level of skill to perform are combined in order to make a dull job seem more interesting (Herzberg, 1968). Often, the average job in sociotechnically designed organizations includes some work that would typically be performed by craft, technical or managerial personnel in a traditional organization.

Medical organizations and universities have long recognized the importance of continued education for their members. As the environments of other organizations become more complex and demanding, the need to promote the development of human resources at all levels has become clearer for them as well. As Ashby's (1960) law dictates, no system can adapt to change without first having the ability to do so; the development of this "requisite variety" through continued education provides a distinct advantage to sociotechnically designed organizations.

3. *Awareness of the external environment.* Organizations which spend an inordinate amount of time "navel gazing" miss important events that indicate change is called for (Aldrich, 1979). If an exclusive focus on internal events is supported for long enough by a munificent environment, organizational leaders may develop a false sense of invulnerability. When the time comes to adapt, the organization may be unprepared to do so, having failed to develop the necessary requisite variety.

Thus, environmental change presents a double-barreled threat to the organization; first, changes which occur may not be recognized; and second, adaptation may be slower than necessary. Sociotechnical systems design encourages environmental awareness by regularly involving employees at all levels in scanning the environment. Key data and information concerning the state of the business, competitors, technogical developments, and social trends are regularly discussed and factored into decision making at all levels.

Ford and Weyerhauser have helped people stay in touch with their suppliers by exchanging some employees with their suppliers for a period of time. Xerox engages in competitive benchmarking, looking at costs for purchasing components from outside vendors and challenging Xerox employees to meet or better those prices in-house. Some Japanese firms post not only their own quarterly results, but those of their competition as well. Procter & Gamble uses focus groups of customers to provide feedback on product quality; Polaroid and Dana hold regular meetings with all employees to discuss the financial state of the business. Tektronix helps improve customer relations by arranging for a customer hotline to ring on the production floor where its oscilloscopes are made; that way, employees get firsthand feedback on their workmanship and customers get helpful information about how to fix their machines.

Regardless of the mechanisms employed, increasing organizational members' awareness of the environment is the first step in gaining their assistance in helping the organization to adapt. Knowledge of the environment sets the problem solving process in motion, which in turn leads to the implementation of ideas which enhance organizational flexibility. Organizations which are more aware of their environments see more opportunities for enhancing their effectiveness than organizations that are less aware; and those that use sociotechnical systems design to transform awareness into actions will outperform those whose structures force them to ignore information indicating that change is necessary.

4. *Maximizing cooperative effort.* Sociotechnical systems design seeks to maximize the use of productive resources in organizations by ensuring that organizational units and actors pursue common goals in a cooperative fashion. At the lowest level, this frequently means designing work and reward systems to encourage group versus individual effort. The autonomous group (Bucklow, 1966; Cummings & Griggs, 1977; Gulwosen, 1979; Goodman & Associates, 1986) has proven a robust and highly effective basic building block for organizational design. Although such groups do vary widely in their true autonomy concerning issues like member selection, member evaluation, work assignment, training, scheduling, selection of technical methods, product development decisions, reward distribution and leadership determination, the fundamental notion of a group of multi-skilled individuals assuming responsibility for a whole piece of work has proven sound across a broad range of applications.

Autonomous groups manage coordination on a real-time basis through informal adjustments among group members rather than relying on supervisors to perform the coordination function. Contrasted with traditional teamwork, in which individuals can perform only specialized tasks, autonomous group members are much more flexible, making cooperation easier. About one-half of all sociotechnical systems experiments involve the establishment of autonomous groups to increase cooperative effort, improve training, heighten motivation, enhance problem solving and improve organizational flexibility (Pasmore et al., 1982).

Where autonomous groups are inappropriate due to skill differentials among team members or where the nature of the work prohibits stable teamwork, alternative means of enchancing cooperation must be employed. Developing common purposes or ideals has long been recognized as an antidote to competitive or conflictual behavior (Sherif, 1966). Beyond common goals, reward systems that emphasize the importance of cooperation can reinforce desired behaviors (Galbraith, 1977). To resolve issues that would otherwise lead to divisive conflict, shared governance systems may be used which invite direct participation in policy making (Simmons & Mares, 1983).

Donnelly Mirrors, for example, uses an "equity committee" structure composed of representatives from all levels of the organization to make decisions about bonus payments under the company's revised Scanlon plan. To encourage cooperation at higher levels, Japanese firms insist that managers rotate through different functional assignments in order to develop a better sense of the acitivities performed by each component of the organization. Union-management cooperation can be enhanced through joint agreements or letters of understanding, as in the case of GM and the UAW.

Again, the objective of maximizing cooperation is to avoid wasting valuable resources through unnecessary duplication of effort, unproductive conflict or working at cross-purposes. Developing autonomous groups, common goals, opportunities for job rotation, innovative reward systems and joint agreements are a few of the ways in which sociotechnical systems design can lead to increased organizational effectiveness.

5. *Developing commitment and energy.* The behavior of organizational members is guided by implicit psychological contracts which specify the amount of effort to be put forth in exchange for the rewards received (Barnard, 1938). The effectiveness of an organization is directly tied to the level of commitment and energy demonstrated by its employees; the psychological contracts between employees and the organization determine the level of energy displayed. Sociotechnical systems design, with its explicit attention to social system dynamics, strives to enhance commitment and energy (Walton, 1985). It does this by enriching the content of work; setting challenging goals; emphasizing shared values; flattening the organizational structure; minimizing status differentials; creating performance-based reward systems; stressing continuous training; involving employees in important decisions; sharing business information; designing work for groups; and enhancing job security.

In the past, much attention has been given to motivating employees under the assumptions that (1) people are somehow motivationally deficient; and (2) that organizations, through a few simple actions, can create motivation where none existed before. Today, we understand more clearly that motivation is always present but not necessarily directed toward organizational goals and that motivation is internally rather than externally controlled (Herzberg, Mausner & Snyderman,

1959). Turning people on to work requires the creating of conditions which allow employees to meet self-determined needs through performing the work itself (Pasmore, 1979).

The issue is *not* one of motivation, but rather of *commitment*; of *directing* motivation, energy and attention toward the accomplishment of organizational goals. Creating the conditions which invoke commitment does not involve changing the person as much as changing the context in which the person works. Shallow gimmicks like employee-of-the-month programs, one-time giveaways, turkeys at Christmas and summer picnics fail to alter the fundamental psychological contract between the individual and organization. Instead, changes in organizational structure, policies, managerial practices, reward systems, work design and other variables are required to generate lasting commitment.

Moreover, it is important that changes aimed at increasing commitment are consistent with one another and the design of the overall system. Incongruities between stated policies and actual behaviors are likely to produce confusion and frustration rather than commitment. To reward employees for team results but restrict them to individual work assignments would lead to dissatisfaction, for example.

At one Buick plant, the desire to make employees more responsible for quality is backed up by the availability of over four hundred buttons which can be used by individual employees to stop the production line if quality problems are detected. At a Packard Electric plant, the same purpose is accomplished by allowing employees to fully test every part they assemble. At Lincoln Electric, Donnelly Mirrors and Herman-Miller, Scanlon plans are used to affirm the assertion that employee commitment to results matters. At DEC's Enfield plant, the desire to make employees responsible for decision making is made clear by the virtual elimination of traditional supervisory positions. At the GM plant in Fitzgerald, Georgia, supervisors exist but are referred to as "coordinators" to signal the fact that their role is to facilitate rather than direct the work of employee groups.

In high commitment organizations, the messages are strong, consistent and clear. Desired behaviors are made explicit and backed up by organizational arrangements that make behaving in traditional ways difficult.

6. *Utilizing social and technical resources effectively.* Sociotechnical systems design is perhaps best known for its focus on joint optimization. Variance analysis provides information pertaining to the most crucial technological problems requiring human control; from the variance analysis, possible changes can be identified which enhance life for employees while resolving technical problems.

Beyond variance analysis, organizations have adopted sociotechnical systems thinking in technological selection and plant design. Volvo's now famous Kalmar plant was designed to enhance the work of autonomous groups. Zilog provided enough technical training to its employees to allow them to participate in redesigning the technical system. A GM plant in Cleveland took employees to visit equipment vendors so that they could influence the design of their technology while it was still on the drawing board. Likewise, in the new Saturn Corporation, technology was not dictated by engineers as it had been in Lordstown a decade earlier; instead, representatives of management and labor worked together to fashion a technology that would create a more rewarding work experience for employees while still being highly efficient.

Once the technology is designed and installed, keeping it going becomes a primary concern. Sociotechnical systems plants in DEC, Gaines, General Foods and Sherwin Williams each employed fewer employees than their traditional counterparts; but machines were kept running at higher levels of efficiency because the employees who operated them were also able to care for them. At one Exxon operation, there are no dedicated maintenance personnel; teams of workers rotate from production into maintenance jobs and back out again.

Large organizations, like LTV and TRW, are finding that smaller plants (less than 200 employees) work better than large ones. Economies of scale turn out to be less than expected as managers find it difficult to control the complex interdependencies in larger operations (Schumacher, 1973).

In summary, sociotechnical systems designs allow organizations to make better use of people and machines. Lower fixed labor costs and less machine downtime translate into competitive advantage in manufacturing settings. In non-manufacturing settings, the same advantages accrue; while equipment running time may not be a prominent factor in organizational effectiveness, proper equipment utilization can be. To the extent that both people and technology are important in achieving success, sociotechnical systems design can lead to significant improvements in organizational performance.

Figure 5-1 summarizes the contrasts between traditional organizational design and sociotechnical systems design.

Appendix A of this book provides a survey instrument which can be used to assess the design of organizations along the six dimensions of innovativeness, human resource development and utilization, environmental agility, cooperation, commitment/energy, and joint optimization. The sociotechnical systems assessment survey (STSAS) may be used prior to redesign to determine which areas are most in need of change or after redesign to determine whether or not the changes made produced the results intended. Interesting comparisons are also possible between managers' and employees' perceptions of the organization. Some of the design features highlighted in the STSAS are discussed in

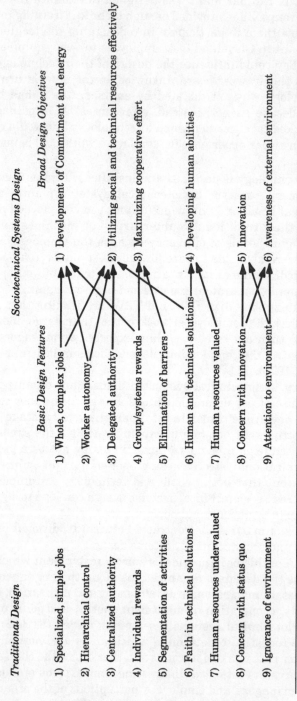

Figure 5-1 Traditional versus Sociotechnical Systems Design

Traditional Design

1) Specialized, simple jobs
2) Hierarchical control
3) Centralized authority
4) Individual rewards
5) Segmentation of activities
6) Faith in technical solutions
7) Human resources undervalued
8) Concern with status quo
9) Ignorance of environment

Sociotechnical Systems Design

Basic Design Features

1) Whole, complex jobs
2) Worker autonomy
3) Delegated authority
4) Group/systems rewards
5) Elimination of barriers
6) Human and technical solutions
7) Human resources valued
8) Concern with innovation
9) Attention to environment

Broad Design Objectives

1) Development of Commitment and energy
2) Utilizing social and technical resources effectively
3) Maximizing cooperative effort
4) Developing human abilities
5) Innovation
6) Awareness of external environment

the next section, which reviews 30 years of sociotechnical systems experimentation all over the world.

Sociotechnical Systems Design: A Review of Practice

Reviews of the sociotechnical systems literature by Friedlander and Brown (1974), Taylor (1977), Walton (1974) and Pasmore et al., (1982) have provided insight into the actual use of various sociotechnical system design features. Although published accounts of sociotechnical systems experiments are often incomplete and may at times be misleading, this literature is our best source of information concerning the actual practice of sociotechnical systems design.

Figure 5-2 depicts the frequency of use of design features across the organizations included in the review. Figure 5-3 reports the results observed when the features were used and results were reported. Although we will discuss the design features independently, it is important to note that the best efforts included in our sample utilized a number of the design features simultaneously in a systemic approach to organizational change. The results reported here cannot separate out the independent effect each design feature had on the bottom line. Hence, when it is said that a design feature "was associated with positive results," it is meant that it was part of an overall effort which produced those results. While it would be advantageous to know the impact of each design feature separately, this is not possible given the way results are typically reported. At the same time, this method of reporting does alert us to cases in which the use of a design feature may have caused bottom line measures to worsen.

The most popular design feature has been the formation of autonomous groups. When these groups were utilized and results were reported, they were associated with improvements in productivity, costs, attitudes, and quality over 80% of the time.

Training to enhance the level of technical knowledge of the work force has been used next most often, in about 40% of the reported cases. In order to be able to control variances at their source, employees must understand both the equipment they use in the conversion process and the process, itself. Improving technical skills enhances trouble-shooting capabilities and also increases the likelihood that operators will be able to offer meaningful suggestions to improve how work is done. Training was associated with improvements in performance in over 90% of the cases which reported its use.

Twenty-two percent of the efforts involved the formation of action groups or task forces to analyze the organization and recommend

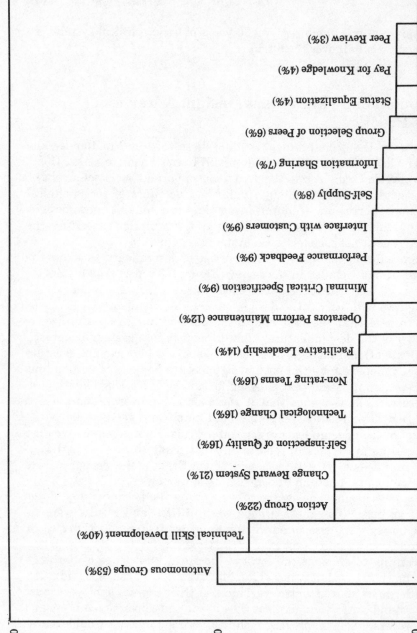

Figure 5-2 Frequency of Usage of Sociotechnical System Design Features in 134 Reported Cases

Peer Review (3%)
Pay for Knowledge (4%)
Status Equalization (4%)
Group Selection of Peers (6%)
Information Sharing (7%)
Self-Supply (8%)
Interface with Customers (9%)
Performance Feedback (9%)
Minimal Critical Specification (9%)
Operators Perform Maintenance (12%)
Facilitative Leadership (14%)
Non-rating Teams (16%)
Technological Change (16%)
Self-inspection of Quality (16%)
Change Reward System (21%)
Action Group (22%)
Technical Skill Development (40%)
Autonomous Groups (53%)

Recent
% Studies
Using this
Feature

100   50   0

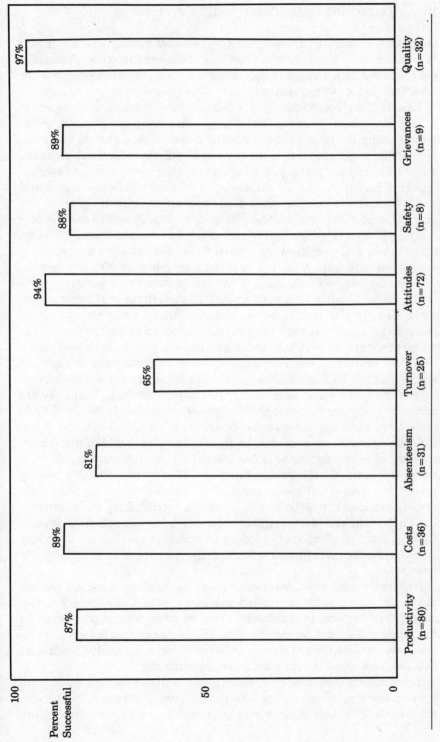

Figure 5-3 Percentage of Studies Reporting Success on Performance Dimensions

changes. Occasionally these groups consisted of managers exclusively; more often, they involved cross-sections of the organization. Productivity improved in all cases in our sample in which action groups were used and results were reported.

Lawler (1981) has discussed the use of reward systems to bring about organization development; 21% of the organizations in our sample reported using changes in their reward systems as a part of their approach. In some cases, this meant moving from individual payment schemes to pay for group performance. In other cases it meant switching from hourly pay to all salaried pay plans for both managers and employees. Given the fact that experimentation with innovative pay plans is a relatively recent phenomenon, we can expect to see the percentage of organizations trying out new pay schemes increase. When undertaken and results were reported, reward system changes were associated with improvements in performance in over 80% of cases.

Allowing workers to inspect their own quality was a feature in 16% of the cases. Quality improved in 92% of the efforts that reported results. Clearly, the traditional assumption that employees cannot be trusted to inspect the work they perform needs to be laid to rest.

Surprisingly, only 16% of the organizations which undertook sociotechnical systems design reported making technological changes. It seems that the bulk of sociotechnical efforts have failed to take advantage of the power technological change can have in changing behaviors and enhancing organizational effectiveness. Apparently, we need to do more to educate and involve the designers of technical systems in sociotechnical systems concepts. In the organizations which did undertake changes in their technical systems and reported results, all were successful in improving quality but only 60% were successful in raising productivity. Again, it seems surprising that new technology does not always produce better bottom-line results, particularly since improving the bottom line is the primary motivation for technological change. Clearly, more work needs to be done to understand what is happening in experiments involving new technology or changes in existing technologies.

Naturally occurring developments in technology, such as the replacement of operator-controlled machines with CAD-CAM devices, should free workers to become involved in more meaningful tasks. In the white-collar and service sectors, office automation offers tremendous possibilities for the reconfiguration of work (Pava, 1983). Failure to seize these opportunities would be unfortunate.

Team approaches to work restructuring, unlike autonomous groups, involve workers who are unable to perform one anothers' jobs but who nevertheless depend upon a stable group of peers in accomplishing goals. In the 16% of organizations that used the team approach, results were quite positive; about 80% of those reporting noted improvements in performance.

Leadership has become a major topic of discussion in the implementation of sociotechnical systems designs (Walton & Schlesinger, 1979; Schlesinger, 1983; Mans & Sims, 1983; Pasmore, Morris & Estavez, 1983; Klein & Posey, 1986). Neverthless, only 14% of the organizations in our sample mentioned specific programs designed to ensure that supervision was facilitative versus directive. More recently, organizations like DEC, GE and Goodyear have begun to experiment with self-directed workforces, in which no first-line supervisors are present. The changing (and disappearing) role of supervisors should continue to be the source of some controversy in sociotechnical systems design.

Employees were encouraged to perform their own maintenance in 12% of the organizations. Productivity improvements were noted in 88% of these cases which also reported results. It was impossible to tell what level of maintenance work was actually performed in these cases, but experience would suggest that few involved the performance of licensed craft work. In several cases, union contracts were amended to allow employees to perform trade work; but concerns about safety and training costs have limited the full development of craft skills by employees in most cases.

Other design features were used in less than 10% of the organizations in the sample. Nevertheless, when they were used, they were almost always associated with improvements in performance.

Minimal critical specification (Walton, 1972; Cherns, 1976) refers to allowing employees to take part in creating as much of the final design as possible, with minimum (but critical) constraints imposed by management. Following this practice tends to produce an organization which is better designed to meet employees' needs and which is less encumbered by needless rules, policies or procedures.

Feedback to employees on their performance was shown to have a uniformly positive effect on performance among the organizations studied here. Feedback is a prerequisite to learning and self-calibration. Unfortunately, many employees work without direct knowledge of their results in terms of either productivity or quality. Managers who receive yearly performance appraisals are no better off; given the low cost of providing feedback, it appears that doing so represents a tremendous opportunity for increasing organizational effectiveness.

Allowing employees to interface directly with customers (customers are those who consume the product or service one makes, whether those customers are internal or external to the organization) increases feelings of task significance and provides additional feedback on performance (Hackman & Oldham, 1980). Again, given the low cost of arranging for this contact to occur in many cases, more use of this feature can be expected.

Self-supply of materials refers to instances in which employees were permitted to acquire inputs for their tasks without having to wait for them to be delivered or to obtain approval from their superiors. This also refers to allowing employees to have access to tool cribs, testing equipment and other support needed to complete a whole job. While not a major feature in terms of its usage, the absence of self-supply can be frustrating in a system which in other ways is geared for high performance.

Status equalization, in which reserved parking spaces, special cafeterias, or other status symbols are done away with to demonstrate the importance of each person's contribution to the organization regardless of their level, occurred in less than 5% of the organizations. The same is true of pay for knowledge, which has already been discussed as important in enriching jobs and helping the organization become more flexible; and of peer review, which places responsibility for performance appraisal on those who work most closely with each other. Each of these features should become more prominent in the future than they have been during the last 35 years of experimentation with sociotechnical systems design.

All of the design features described can be used separately or in conjunction with one another. Again, the best efforts take a systemic perspective and use many of these features in creating innovative, high performance work settings.

Summary

The sociotechnical systems principles outlined in this chapter present guidelines for creating effective organizations. A review of sociotechnical systems experimentation reveals that these principles are being followed, but that some design features are currently underutilized. Of course, each organization is unique, and therefore should develop a design that best fits its own internal and external environment.

Choosing the proper sociotechnical systems design is important; but it is equally important that the process of choosing the design be carried out in a way which enhances the commitment of organizational members to making it work. The next chapter discusses the methods that have been developed to facilitate sociotechnical systems redesign.

CHAPTER SIX

Sociotechnical Systems Redesign

Few organizational change efforts are as far-reaching and complex as sociotechnical systems redesign. Virtually every aspect of an organization may be affected; and while each change represents an opportunity for improvement, each may also be the source of some resistance. Because it is so complex, sociotechnical systems redesign calls for careful planning, widespread involvement, adequate resources, strong management support and skillful facilitation.[1]

The model presented here is based on a number of important assumptions regarding the circumstances surrounding the redesign effort. First, it is assumed that the target system is already in existence and is being redesigned. This assumption is made because redesign situations require greater preparation than new designs or "greenfield" situations as they are sometimes called. While the same steps should be followed in greenfield situations, many of the difficulties arising from historical modes of operation will be avoided.

Second, it is assumed that the redesign effort involves either an internal or external consultant who acts as a third party to labor-management discussions and provides expert guidance during the change process. In the absence of skilled consultants to facilitate the process, managers will need to take extra care in educating themselves about the sociotechnical systems approach and be especially sensitive to power imbalances between themselves and their subordinates during the change effort.

---

[1] The model for sociotechnical systems design outlined in this chapter is an evolution of earlier versions proposed by Foster (1967) and Cummings (1976) and is intended for use by managers or consultants interested in undertaking comprehensive sociotechnical systems redesign. My thanks to Abraham Shani for his help in developing an earlier draft of this model.

Third, it is assumed that the redesign process itself should reflect the values of sociotechnical systems; that is, that the change process should serve as a model for the type of participation in decision making that is expected after the organization is redesigned. The model presented here is based upon a high involvement change strategy, rather than one in which an expert works exclusively with top management to determine what changes are necessary.

Finally, it is presumed that the unit being redesigned is part of a larger system which both supports the redesign process and places constraints upon it. In situations where the target of change is a whole organization, some of the steps in the model which deal with managing corporate relations may be safely bypassed.

The model discussed in this chapter is designed to maximize the likelihood that significant changes will result from the effort put into sociotechnical systems redesign. It is not a quick-fix, limited scope, cosmetic process which is tightly controlled by management alone. If followed as outlined here, the model may take anywhere from six months to three years to complete; it will probably demand full-time attention by several organizational members, require a substantial outlay of resources, and call into question every aspect of the organization's design and operating practices; moreover, it is almost certain to disrupt organizational performance for a period of time. But in the end, it is more likely to produce changes that are desired–and often demanded–in a competitive environment.

An Overview of the Change Model

As indicated in Figure 6-1, there are nine major steps in the model. Each of them is described briefly and then followed later by a more complete explanation.

Step 1: Define the scope of the system to be redesigned.

The first step in the sociotechnical systems change process is intended to clarify the boundaries of the organizational unit to be redesigned. In addition, it includes the activities associated with the entry, scouting and contracting phases in typical organization development efforts. These include defining the need for change, determining the potential for success, agreeing on a change model (in this case, the sociotechnical systems change model presented here), defining rough time and cost parameters, clarifying expectations among parties, forming a steering committee to oversee the effort, and agreeing to a public contract which outlines the work to be done.

Step 2: Determine environmental demands.

The second step in the change process involves identifying important constituencies in the external environment who might impact the

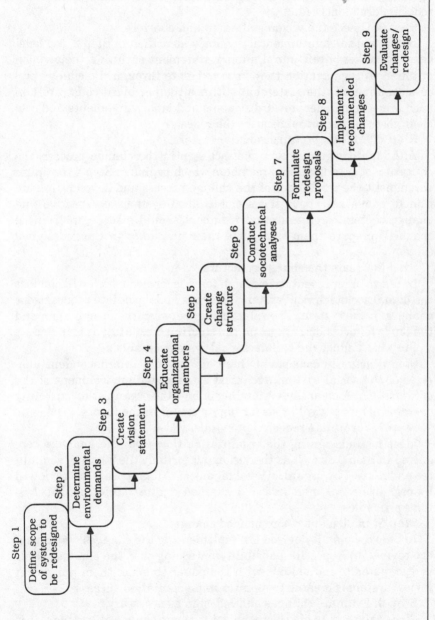

Figure 6-1 Sociotechnical Systems Change Model

Step 1
Define scope
of system to
be redesigned

Step 2
Determine
environmental
demands

Step 3
Create
vision
statement

Step 4
Educate
organizational
members

Step 5
Create
change
structure

Step 6
Conduct
sociotechnical
analyses

Step 7
Formulate
redesign
proposals

Step 8
Implement
recommended
changes

Step 9
Evaluate
changes/
redesign

nature and scope of changes that will occur in the organization. Based on the perceived demands of competitors, shareholders, corporate management and others, areas of opportunity as well as constraints on the redesign are identified.

Step 3: Create the vision statement and charter.

Based on the environmental demands identified in Step 2, top level decision makers draft a preliminary statement outlining their vision of the ideal organization they hope to create through the change process. In addition, the statement outlines the perceived constraints in such areas as policies, reward systems and labor agreements and sets clear goals for performance after the redesign.

Step 4: Educate organizational members.

Although designated as a distinct step in the change process, the education of organizational members which begins in Step 4 continues throughout the remainder of the change process and beyond. In addition to education about the sociotechnical systems perspective and change process, organizational members should also begin training that will prepare them to assume their new roles in the redesigned system.

Step 5: Create the change structure.

In Step 5, a representative design team is formed which will conduct the actual sociotechnical systems analysis and formulate proposals for changes in the system. The relationship between the design team and the top level decision makers on the steering committee is clarified.

Step 6: Conduct the sociotechnical systems analysis.

Step 6 actually consists of three distinct but interdependent analyses of the social system, technical system, and environment of the organization. A clear understanding of how the organization currently operates points toward areas for improvement in the future.

Step 7: Formulate redesign proposals.

Ideas for redesigning the organization flow from the analyses conducted in Step 6 as well as the vision put forth by the steering committee and revised by organizational members. All proposals are reviewed by organizational members and checked against sociotechnical systems principles.

Step 8: Implement recommended changes.

In Step 8 a plan is devised for implementing the changes which pass the review in Step 7. Responsibility for seeing that the changes occur is designated to individuals with the power to make them happen. A review system is created to monitor implementation success.

Step 9: Evaluate changes and redesign as necessary.

Since the process of sociotechnical systems change is complex, it is necessary to evaluate the changes that are made to ascertain whether they are producing their intended effects. The adjustment of the organization to its changing environment demands that the redesign process recurs on a regular basis.

Each of these steps will now be reviewed in greater detail, using illustrations from actual sociotechnical systems change efforts.

Define the Scope of the System To Be Redesigned

It's difficult to say precisely in which step most unsuccessful sociotechnical systems change efforts fail; but when efforts do fail, it is not uncommon to hear those involved say, "We knew from the beginning that this wouldn't work here." The lesson to be learned is that the amount of time and effort taken to define the parameters of the change effort before proceeding is small compared to the potential time wasted if a partially completed effort is later abandoned.

A common error is beginning with a small pilot experiment in the hope that once the pilot proves successful, the changes tried there can be diffused to the larger system. This seldom happens. Pilot experiments tend not to be good examples for a couple of reasons. First, they are seldom as successful as they are expected to be because the larger system sets too many constraints on the pilot, restricting innovations that might allow it to succeed. Second, even when successful, pilot experiments are regarded as unique examples not directly comparable to large scale operations, and therefore as poor guides for system-wide change. Instead of pilot experiments, the target of change should be a whole product or process with organizational integrity. Organizational integrity means that the unit to be redesigned should encompass all or most of the operations needed to transform inputs into outputs and be able to modify its structure, policies, and processes without undue intereference from the larger system of which it is a part.

The steps involved in defining the scope of the system to be redesigned and clarifying the parameters of the change effort are listed in Figure 6-2.

Define the need for change. Unless the desired outcomes of the change effort are clear, there may not be sufficient support to continue the process during times of adversity. Sociotechnical systems design efforts should not be undertaken lightly; unless managers have a clear desire for significant improvement (30% or more) they will probably back down when crucial changes are suggested. Redesign efforts need to be driven by a demand for the organization to improve—not just by doing more of the same a little better. Managers who are looking for "another personnel program" will probably be dismayed by the complexity and farreaching changes suggested by the sociotechnical systems change process.

Defining the Scope of the System to be Redesigned

- Define the need for change
- Define the target organization
- Identify the key stakeholders
- Determine the stakeholder's expectations
- Determine potential for success
- Form steering committee
- Agree on change model
- Define rough parameters of the change effort
- Clarify expectations among parties
- Finalize contract

Figure 6-2 Defining the Scope of the System to be Redesigned

In the case of an oil refining company, the CEO was reluctant to enter into a redesign of his whole organization at one time, despite the obvious pressure he was under to cut costs in the face of falling crude oil prices. He was hesitant to risk the disruption that an all-out effort could produce and instead opted for an experiment in the organization's utilities department. The utilities department was a relatively self-contained unit which transformed inputs (fuel) into outputs (electricity, steam) and could be reorganized independently. In making his decision, the CEO was aware that he was trading off getting a pilot started quickly with possible problems in diffusing the results of the pilot to the rest of the organization in the long run. The pilot is still underway and it remains unclear whether or not diffusion will take place in this case.

Define the target organization. In some cases, the need for change is clear but the place to begin is not. Large corporations, for example, are often faced with choices regarding which units should undertake redesign efforts first. In the past, several organizations have chosen new plants as the sites for experimentation with new designs, since it is generally easier to start from scratch than to change existing arrangements. While effective in the short run, the strategy of beginning with greenfield sites has been shown to create some problems for diffusion later on. The Topeka, Kansas plant in General Foods and the Lima, Ohio plant in Procter & Gamble operated successfully for many years before other units began to accept and adopt their methods of operation.

At the other extreme, it's wise to avoid operations that are failing badly or have a history of severe labor-management conflict. Often, failing operations lack the resources and conditions to sustain a long-term, intensive redesign effort. In some cases, these operations can be saved; but they tend to make difficult places to begin experimenting with innovative ways of working.

Thus, existing operations which are functioning well but could improve further represent the best starting point for successful redesign and diffusion. In one photographic corporation, redesign was begun at multiple locations, including the company's most advanced and crucial manufacturing facility. The fact that corporate leaders were supportive of experimentation in a plant that was already regarded as one of the company's best sent a signal throughout the company that management was serious about using sociotechnical systems methods to improve organizational effectiveness.

Identify key stakeholders. Key stakeholders are those who can influence the success of the redesign effort. They include groups like corporate management, middle managers, employees, and the skilled trades. At this point in the redesign process, the concern is with groups internal to the organization; later, attention will be given to the external environment.

Determine stakeholder's expectations. Once the question of who can impact the success of the redesign is answered, the next question is, "What do these groups need to see happen in order for them to help make the change process a success?". The answers to this question are inherently political, having to do with issues of power and equity.

In the case of a health care organization, a redesign effort in the medical laboratory included physicians, administrators and laboratory technicians as the key stakeholder groups. The expectations of physicians (to retain ultimate control over decision making) were in conflict with those of technicians (to be more directly involved in patient care and make more independent decisions concerning the tests they ran). When such conflicts are identified early, steps can be taken to deal with them constructively or to reconsider the wisdom of proceeding with the redesign.

Determine the potential for success. Once the demands of the stakeholder groups are known, an assessment can be made of the chances that the redesign will meet their demands. In the health care laboratory just mentioned, the chances for success were viewed as slim unless either the physicians or technicians were willing to alter their demands.

In addition, a rough assessment should be made to determine whether the organization can support the intensity of the redesign process. Are resources available to support the analysis and redesign? Are changes in policies, structures, and systems possible? Can the technical system be altered if necessary? Is the environment too threatening for risk taking to occur? Do leaders share the values of participation and equity that underlie the approach? Is leadership stable? Is there sufficient trust between labor and management to permit frank discussions and widespread involvement?

Form steering committee. If the decision is to proceed, a group of top level decision makers should sanction the redesign effort. In the case of one GM plant, the steering committee consisted of the top level plant staff and their union counterparts, since both groups were regarded as key decision makers concerning the redesign. In the photographic products company, one plant's steering committee included a corporate vice president and an hourly employee in an attempt to maintain ties across the levels of the organization.

The functions of the steering committee are to authorize experimentation and to review results against internal and external expectations. The steering committee is the link between corporate management and the design team; it makes decisions concerning which recommendations to implement and provides continuing support for the redesign process.

Agree on change model. Questions to be addressed during this phase include: "Will there be broad or narrow participation in the redesign?"; "Should we follow the sociotechnical systems model, or would something else be better?"; and, "What roles should key stakeholders play in the process?". Again, the model presented here is best suited to situations in which managers are open to input from employees, the desired change is comprehensive and stakeholders are prepared to commit a significant amount of time and energy to the change effort.

Define rough parameters of the redesign. How long should it take? How much will it cost? How many people should be involved? There are no predetermined answers to these and other similar questions; the answers must be found by striking a realistic balance between the theoretical ideals of infinite time, unlimited resources, and total involvement and the limitations posed by the actual situation. Few of us would contract with an architect to build a house if we didn't know how long it would take to build it, how much it would cost or how many rooms it would have. But in sociotechnical systems redesign, the answers to these simple questions are not always clear. Much depends on the amount of time managers are willing to devote to the redesign effort; the complexity of the social and technical systems; the changes that are recommended after the analyses; the degree of interference from external groups; the consultant's availability; the time it takes to arrange educational seminars and visits to other organizations; the scope of the effort; production demands; the degree of resistance encountered; the extent of disruption from concurrent changes in technology or personnel; and the pressure from Wall Street to show a profit the next quarter.

Although experiences vary widely (anywhere from six months to nine years) most would indicate that typical redesign efforts take between 18 months and three years. We live in an age of instant everything; some managers are unaccustomed to deciding to do something and then being told that they will have to wait more than a year to see the results of their decision. The problem with being too optimistic about the time frame is that support may evaporate as deadlines are passed without visible signs of progress. Again, the redesign effort should be viewed as a long term investment rather than as a quick fix.

Clarify expectations among parties. When asked about corporate headquarter's role in the redesign, one plant manager told me, "I'd prefer that they know as little as possible about what we are doing. They'll just stick their noses in and screw things up." While he was right about his manager's propensity to get too involved in the details of what was happening in his plant, the plant manager was naive to think that he could hide the change effort from his boss. His hope was that changes could be made before his conservative superiors could disapprove them; but to be successful, redesign efforts usually call for changes in policies, practices and structural arrangements which require corporate approval.

In the long run, it pays for all of the key stakeholders to be in agreement about the nature and scope of the redesign, even if it means some delay on the front end of the process to obtain consensus. When consensus is impossible, it's up to managers to be aware of the risks they are facing and decide whether or not to gamble with their resources and careers.

Finalize the contract. Once the conditions and parameters of the redesign are understood, it's usually helpful to finalize and publicize the agreements that have been made. Written contracts, while not necessarily binding in this situation, serve as helpful reminders of intentions and expectations. Later, when these agreements are referred to, stakeholders can challenge each other to live up to the stated goals of the redesign.

Determine Environmental Demands

Every organization is an open system, as discussed in Chapter 2. In redesigning an organization, it is important to recognize that both constraints and opportunities are presented by the external environment. The steps involved in determining environmental demands are listed in Figure 6-3.

Determine Environmental Demands

- Identify key external stakeholders
- Determine current and future stakeholder demands
- Decide on appropriate responses to demands
- Derive organizational goals

Figure 6-3 Determine Environmental Demands

Identify external stakeholders. External stakeholders are individuals, groups or organizations that could be affected by the outcomes of the redesign and in turn could affect the way in which the redesigned organization would operate. *Key* external stakeholders are those whose demands could affect the organization most significantly. In this phase of the process, the primary concern is with these key stakeholders. In a food processing plant, key stakeholders included corporate management, the international union and competitors, among others.

Determine current and future stakeholder demands. The demands of the key stakeholders are discussed and clarified. Steering committee members are usually aware of these demands; but if additional information is required, it is better to obtain it at this point than to discover it by chance later on. And while future demands cannot be predicted precisely, the redesign should not violate the anticipated expectations of key stakeholders or fail to seize opportunities the future may offer.

The food processing plant steering committee recognized that the demands of its corporate stakeholder group were for low cost, high quality output; meeting production schedules; maintaining good labor relations; and flexibility during product changeovers. These demands were forecast to remain the same or even intensify in the future. The demands of the international union were for conformance to contract provisions, increased pay and benefits for its members, and enhanced employment stability. Competitors were exerting pressure on the organization to lower its prices, innovate technologically, and introduce products more rapidly.

Decide on appropriate responses to demands. Once identified, the demands of the key external stakeholders are reviewed and appropriate responses to them developed. The basic choices available are to: (1) agree with the demand and try to meet or even exceed it; (2) ignore it and run the risk of losing stakeholder support; or (3) disagree with it and attempt to influence the stakeholder to alter or drop it.

Members of the food processing plant's steering committee agreed with the demands of corporate management and felt that the redesign would help the organization meet these demands with greater effectiveness. The steering committee disagreed with some of the demands of the international union and sought to change them through discussions with the international representative. Specifically, the steering committee felt that in order to experiment with new work designs, it would need more flexibility than the current contract provided; in addition, the steering committee felt that the demand for higher pay might have to be ignored in the short run, or at least not associated with the redesign effort. In exchange, the steering committee, with corporate backing, was prepared to make firmer commitments in the area of future employment stability. The organization accepted the challenges posed by its competition as well.

Often, an organization will be confronted with conflicting demands by its various stakeholders. Under such circumstances, the steering committee can decide for itself which demands it chooses to meet, or bring the stakeholders together in an attempt to achieve consensus among them.

Derive organizational goals. The projected external demands, together with the organization's responses to them, provide further clarification of the goals for the redesign effort. Some goals are merely reaffirmed (high quality) while others are introduced (employment stability) or dropped (match every product introduced by competitors).

Create Vision Statement

Figure 6-4 lists the major steps in creating the vision and charter statements. The vision statement is an expression of the values underlying the effort and a statement of its intended outcomes. The charter contains marching orders for those carrying out the redesign effort.

State philosophy, clarify values and outcomes, draft statement. Successful sociotechnical systems redesign requires that managers hold theory Y assumptions about people (McGregor, 1960). The vision statement proclaims publicly that management intends to recreate the organization to fit with theory Y assumptions and other important values. Later, the vision statement will serve as a standard by which day-to-day operating decisions are made. When new employees are hired, technical processes introduced, or new reward systems considered, the question raised should be, "Does this course of action fit with the vision statement and with our assumptions about people?"

The vision statement should also clarify intended social and economic benefits of the redesign, setting challenging but attainable goals for short-term improvement and long-run success. Sample vision statements from two actual efforts are shown in Figures 6-5 and 6-6.

```
┌─────────────────────────────────────────────────────────────┐
│                                                               │
│     Create  Vision  Statement  and  Charter                  │
│                                                               │
├─────────────────────────────────────────────────────────────┤
│                                                               │
│          •  State philosophy and values                      │
│          •  Clarify desired outcomes                         │
│          •  Draft vision statement                           │
│          •  Charter the change effort                        │
│          •  Review above with sponsors                       │
│                                                               │
└─────────────────────────────────────────────────────────────┘
```

Figure 6-4 Create Vision Statement and Charter

Vision Statement

We work in a plant where pride, ownership, employment security and trust are a way of life. We are admired and respected by the corporation; envied and feared by our competitors. We hold a special position in the global workplace; our products work *every time*! We are *the leader* in our industry.

We manufacture many highly technical, versatile and innovative products that have captured the imagination of our customers. We work hand-in-hand with research to develop the highest quality, unique and manufacturable systems. *Quality* is owned by all employees and will always remain the number one goal in what we do. Productivity and yield are the highest they have ever been and we challenge ourselves to improve even more.

We are the leaders in creating a safe and clean workplace. We care about a clean environment and the community in which we live and work. The contributions to the community by the plant and our employees are varied and valued by all. We have attained our #1 position by sharing common goals and by being more creative than our competitors, both technically and socially.

We encourage and reward both individual and team contributions. Our enduring culture brings out the best in us and is one of challenge, innovation, excellence, respect and friendship. Work is characterized by a feeling of cooperation, flexibility, satisfaction, accomplishment, high energy and fun. Important business decisions are made at all levels of the organization.

We are all proactive in the operation of the plant, our jobs and careers through lifelong learning. Information flows freely throughout our company. We encourage and reward risk taking. We evaluate ourselves on how well we help each other succeed. We are self-sufficient in many ways yet are productively linked to the rest of the corporation.

We are proud of what we have accomplished. To change, evolve and excel in a dynamic environment, we look forward to the future with energy, excitement and enthusiasm.

Figure 6-5 Sample Vision Statement

Mission Statement

Our mission is *job security* and *job satisfaction* for all employees. To accomplish this mission and create new jobs, we manufacture world class products which are competitive in the world market in *quality, reliability, performance and profitability* using the following principles:

Personal Responsibility
1. Everyone is treated with fairness, respect and dignity.
2. Assure effective and meaningful training for everyone.
3. Everyone takes responsibility and pride in maintaining a clean, safe environment.
4. Each individual accepts ownership for the outcomes of their work, and assists others to assure the success of the system.
5. Every individual's principal goal is customer satisfaction.
6. Everyone measures their actions against this philosophy.

Management's Role
7. Provide the following: well defined objectives; necessary resources; minimum interference; support self-management.
8. Support a work system in which: operating decisions are made as close to the point of action as possible; creativity and innovation are encouraged; customer needs are met in a flexible and responsive manner.

Awareness
9. Each individual is responsible for communications (both listening and talking) in an honest, open and understandable manner.
10. High levels of commitment and individual responsibility are promoted through continuous sharing of information on all aspects of the business.
11. Trust and performance are enhanced by constructive and continuous feedback throughout the organization.

Common Objectives and Teamwork
12. All levels of union and management work together effectively to achieve common objectives.
13. *All* individuals and *all* functions that touch the product are committed to support the common objectives of the system, forming a united team effort. In addition, each is committed to learning from the other.
14. Performance improvements are openly recognized and actively supported.
15. Rewards promote this philosophy.

Follow-up
16. This living philosophy, as well as the work design, is continually measured, reviewed, and updated to assure our success.

Figure 6-6 Sample Mission Statement

Charter the change effort. The charter defines the process to be used in redesigning the organization more clearly as well as the constraints on design outcomes. Its purpose is to instruct those involved in redesign activities; it is not a permanent document as is the vision statement. An effective charter describes the change model (in this case the sociotechnical systems change model); sets the time frame within which the redesign should be completed; clarifies expected outcomes; identifies the resources available for people to work with; sets minimum constraints on outcomes; states decision making procedures (who makes the final decisions about the design, and what opportunity is there to influence those decisions?); and sets checkpoints at which redesign progress will be reviewed.

Once the broad parameters of the charter are defined, the charter should be reviewed with corporate sponsors to ensure their understanding and support for the redesign process. Sample charters from two redesign efforts are illustrated in Figures 6-7 and 6-8.

Educate Organizational Members

Sociotechnical systems education. Prior to moving ahead with the formation of a design team, the steering committee needs to devise a plan for educating organizational members about the redesign process. Elements to be covered include but are not limited to: reasons for the change; the vision; sociotechnical systems concepts; steps in the change process; the change structure (including the role of the union, if one exists); opportunities for participation in the redesign process; how the process will affect job assignments, responsibilities and job security; communication plans; the timeframe; plans for additional education; and next steps to be taken.

The educational effort signals the importance of the redesign effort and begins the flow of open information between the steering committee and the rest of the organization. Based upon the education they receive, organizational members can make better choices concerning their own level of involvement and about who can best represent their interests on the design team.

Skill training. Opportunities for enhancing skills should be made available as early as possible. Creating a high performance organization requires educating organizational members to assume more meaningful roles and a broader range of responsibilities. The sooner this is accomplished, the quicker the benefits of the redesign will be realized.

In addition to technical skill training, training in the areas of communication, interpersonal dynamics, problem solving, and leadership is helpful. All members of the organization (including the steering committee) should receive this training; in high performing organizations, ongoing learning is a regular part of everyone's job.

Charter

Design Team's Role

Meet the requirements of the charter and function within its parameters; work *with* the steering committee; represent the entire organization – not just your individual views – in the technical and social considerations; be responsible to ensure that a more optimal work structure is created through communication with and participation of the entire organization; recognize the importance of your role; learn sociotechnical systems and be able to sell its outcomes; be a positive model to the organization; self-appraise and critique both quality and progress; constantly communicate with the organization; steward progress and problems to the steering committee; work to make the acceptance of the design easy; assist in implementation; work hard, our collective future depends on it.

Expected Outcomes

Improved product quality; higher work satisfaction; increased sense of responsibility; increased flexibility; legitimate employment security; pay and rewards consistent with company and individual objectives; improved productivity; increased technical competence; adoption of change as a natural part of doing business; innovation.

Desirable Outcomes (Human)

One class of employee, eliminating arbitrary boundaries between members; a place where one comes to work for more than just the dollars; a place where jobs are challenging, fun and envied by other divisions; individual control over work assignments; everyone has the chance to experience the pleasure of individual achievement; a place that fosters team effort and spirit; a place embracing lifelong learning; a place that encourages creativity and risk taking in the development of ideas and eliminates the fear of expressing them.

Desirable Outcomes (Organizational)

Delegation to its lowest and most effective level; a flexible workforce that by itself moves easily to where the work needs to be done; fewer job classifications; fewer levels of management; working safely is a part of the culture; an organization that can evolve its design and practices with little turmoil so that it will always stay ahead of the competition.

Desirable Outcomes (Business)

Being the industrial equivalent of a world champion sports team; make product introductions in half the time and with higher quality; develop the ability to plan ahead and avoid problems instead of reacting to them; hire and develop people with tomorrow in mind; increase communication of business information for all; develop a rapid grievance procedure or eliminate the need; productivity that is double today's by 1990; be able to handle increased productivity and product variety while maintaining quality; establish a "no defects" philosophy; establish and maintain 95% + yields in processing; implement the future technology agenda; lower costs.

Constraints

Must use the sociotechnical systems process; must satisfy the "expected" outcomes; discretion allowed only on "desirable" outcomes; proposed changes and final design will require approval by the steering committee; must be compatible with stated corporate philosophy; must fit with new corporate compensation program; cannot disrupt production; must maintain safe working conditions during and after change; company benefits are non-negotiable; must enhance equal opportunity and embrace human differences; design team must operate within budget; must follow and meet redesign schedule; must respect employee seniority but not be restricted by it. The design team should not make the mistake of assuming there are other constraints without thoroughly testing them.

Figure 6-7 Sample Design Team Charter

Steering Team's Charge to the Design Team

Design Team's Charge

1. *Learn* about innovative and high performing work designs through workshops and visits to other companies and plants where such systems are being used.
2. Develop a *statement of philosophy or vision statement* specifying the principles which are to govern the new work organization and your work as a design team.
3. Conduct an *environmental analysis* of the manufacturing system to determine the complete set of expectations which others will impose on this organization.
4. Analyze the *social system* within which the new manufacturing system will operate.
5. Analyze the *technical system* which has been proposed and suggest modifications as appropriate to achieve the best fit between technology, the people who will operate it, and the environment.
6. Make specific *recommendations* to the steering committee on (a) the design of jobs; (b) the work flow; (c) the work organization, including supply, support and management functions.
7. By October 1, a pilot manufacturing process is to be in place.
8. Maintain *communications* with both the steering team and the remainder of the division while you are working.

Constraints and Limitations on Design Team's Recommendations

1. Your recommendations must meet (a) customer requirements; (b) delivery schedules; (c) costs; (d) quality; (e) reliability; and (f) product specifications.
2. Any plant environmental recommendation must be in keeping with the vision. Avoid cosmetic changes.
3. Any changes must meet contract provisions in effect at the time.
4. Your recommendations must be compatible with current programs and systems, such as the new quality control program.
5. All changes must meet the tests of practicality and economic limitations.
6. Since serving on the design team and making recommendations for improvement is your full time job, you will not be eligible for suggestion awards.

Concerns of the Steering Team

1. The recommendations of the design team will not be supported by others.
2. The remainder of the division will view the design team as elites.

Figure 6-8 Sample Design Team Charter

3. The magnitude and complexity of the design team's assignment.
4. The design team may not think systemically enough, and may overlook important parts of any work system such as the reward system, selection, supply, management structure, etc.
5. The design team needs to share information widely and educate others at the same time you are doing your design work.
6. There may be unproductive conflict within the design team.

Hopes and Aspirations for the Design Team

The steering team hopes for creative and successful work by the design team, which will suggest changes in the technology, the contract, and division/corporate policies, wherever changes are needed to produce the most effective work organization.

Fears for the Design Team

1. Failure.
2. You will simply endorse the design engineers' plans.
3. You will not recommend policy changes or contract changes.
4. There is insufficient time for the design team to do a complete and successful job.
5. Management may not be ready for the challenges the design team will present.
6. The design team may be used by others.
7. This process may undermine union and/or management leadership.
8. The design team will turn into "gophers" and either do errands for management or ignore the world around yourselves.
9. The design team will develop an elitist attitude which will distance you from the people you are serving.

Figure 6-8 (Continued)

Creating the Change Structure

The change structure is a three-party system, as depicted in Figure 6-9. The three parties (steering committee, design team, consultant) each have specific roles to play in the process and serve as checks and balances for one another.

The steering committee oversees the effort, provides resources, sanctions changes and ensures that redesign suggestions are implemented. The design team carries out the sociotechnical systems analyses, makes redesign suggestions and acts as a vehicle for involving organizational members in the redesign process. The consultant provides guidance

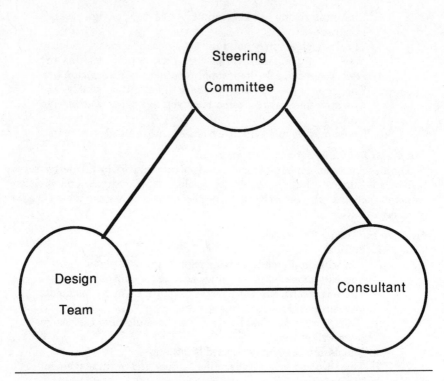

Figure 6-9 The Change Structure

concerning the change process, information about what has been tried elsewhere, and training.

The dynamics of the interactions among the parties affect the outcomes of the design process. If the dynamics are healthy (open communication, frequent engagement, shared values and goals, a willingness to challenge and learn), the outcomes of the effort will be superior to those instances in which the dynamics become unhealthy (the steering committee fails to stay involved; the design team sees its role as overthrowing the steering committee; communication is infrequent; historical conflict overshadows constructive work on the future; the consultant is too detached). The dynamics are influenced by the way the change structure is created and while unhealthy dynamics can never be precluded, the steps outlined in Figure 6-10 help to minimize the chances that they will occur.

Create the design team. The design team is a multi-purpose change vehicle. Its functions include: to analyze the organization's environment, social system and technical system; to suggest how the organi-

```
Create the Change Structure

  • Educate organizational members
  • Create the design team
  • Hold intergroup meeting between design team and steering committee
  • Develop communication strategy
  • Educate design team and steering committee
  • Develop involvement strategy
  • Develop resourcing strategy
  • Develop change strategy
```

Figure 6-10   Create the Change Structure

zation should be redesigned; to act as a representative body for all parts
and levels of the organization; to challenge tradition and conservatism;
to assist in educating others about the redesign process; to communicate information about the process and the redesign; to help plan for
implementation of changes; and to participate in evaluating the
changes and revising them as necessary.

To accomplish all of this, the design team should be composed of a
representative cross section of organizational members. Overlapping
membership with the steering committee by one or two design team
members will help the communication between the two groups. The
bulk of design team members, however, should be chosen from the lower
levels of the organization, to better represent the larger number of people found there and to balance the power of higher level members of
the team. While the design team is not a decision-making body, its
recommendations can be skewed if its internal dynamics are not carefully monitored.

Criteria for membership vary, but certainly include a sincere interest in helping the organization to improve; a willingness to learn; a
desire to participate actively; communication skills; and comfort with
risk-taking. As a whole, the team should reflect the demographics as
well as the politics of the organization. Optimally, its members should
serve full-time; and its size should be the minimum number of people
needed to represent the important interest groups and levels in the
organization (preferably between 7 and 15 members). Leadership in the
team is shared, so that it reflects in its own working the aspects of the
organization it is trying to create.

Selecting design team members is a political process, since it will be viewed differently by different constituencies within the organization, each of which would prefer to see its own method of selection followed. Paying attention to these politics is important, since selecting the design team is one of the first visible acts associated with the redesign process.

Recognizing that some form of participation in the selection is important, the question becomes one of balancing the desire to have the best qualified people on the team with the possibility that if elected, the most popular but not necessarily best qualified people will be chosen. How the selection process is handled says a lot about the future; and regardless of which process is followed, some groups will probably be uncomfortable. In the case of unionized organizations, support for the design team will depend on whether or not design team members reflect union preferences. Involving the union and other stakeholder groups in discussion of the selection process can help to alleviate some of the mistrust that the process can engender.

Once members are selected, the first order of business is to develop the individuals into a team. Team building (Dyer, 1987) is a well established organization development method that can be used for this purpose. Outputs of the team building process should include an understanding of the team's objectives, clarification of how the team will work together to accomplish those objectives, agreements on the roles to be held by team members, and the development of skills in observing how well members are working together (Schein, 1987).

Hold intergroup meeting between design team and steering committee. The first meeting between the steering committee and the design team is important in terms of setting the stage for future interactions. The steering committee should review its thinking behind the charter and consider questions or disagreements raised by the design team. Techniques for managing intergroup meetings are discussed by Walton (1987).

Develop communication strategy. With the first meeting of the design team, curiosity will begin to grow about what the team is up to. The stakes are high; if preliminary talk is true, the design team will transform the organization in ways that affect everyone in it significantly. Consequently, every individual has a vested interest in how the design team operates, what it discusses and what it decides. Therefore, the first action the team needs to consider is designing a strategy for letting others know what it is doing. Frequent, high quality communication (preferably in the form of direct exchange whenever possible) is vital to maintaining involvement and commitment by those who must accept and live with design decisions.

Educate the design team and steering committee. The design team must become familiar with sociotechnical systems concepts and the details of the redesign process. Classroom training is helpful here, but needs to be supplemented by visits to other organizations, discussions with participants in other redesign efforts, attendance at educational conferences and other educational opportunities. Each visit and educational experience should be carefully planned by the design team to maximize potential learning benefits.

The steering committee should participate in the educational activities with the design team. The steering committee needs to be an active participant in the redesign process; complete delegation of the redesign to the design team will create extreme separation between the two groups and hamper the development and implementation of changes in the organization.

Develop involvement strategy. Beyond communication, there is a need to keep others directly involved in the redesign process. Direct involvement increases understanding and acceptance of changes. Furthermore, the design team will need the cooperation of organizational members in conducting its analyses. The involvement strategy identifies who should be involved in what and when, as well as how involvement should be obtained.

Develop resourcing strategy. To become involved, organizational members must have free time; either resources need to be provided to replace them, or overtime pay must be made available, or production/ service levels must be temporarily reduced. The cost of involvement can be high (Pacific Bell spent $40 million last year on salaries and temporary replacements to cover the cost of involving its employees in just one training program) but it is the only way to ensure commitment to the redesign effort.

Develop change strategy. The design team should consider the politics of the change process, identifying what needs to be done to gain the support of various stakeholders. Then, strategies should be devised to obtain buy-in and minimize unnecessary resistance. If it chooses, the design team can record information about the stakeholder groups as illustrated in Figure 6-11.

Conduct Sociotechnical Systems Analyses

This step, carried out by the design team with assistance from others, involves analyzing the environment, social system and technical system as outlined in Chapters 2, 3, and 4 and summarized in Figure 6-12. The purpose of the analyses is to determine where opportunities for improvement lie and to ensure that critical aspects of the organization that make it successful are preserved.

Identify resources to assist in the analyses. Depending on the scope of the effort and the degree of detail desired in the analyses, the design team may require help in completing its assessment of the system. In

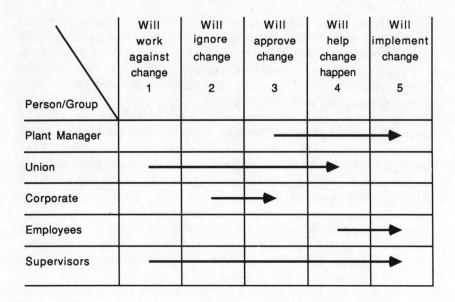

Person/Group	Will work against change 1	Will ignore change 2	Will approve change 3	Will help change happen 4	Will implement change 5
Plant Manager			→————————→		→
Union	→————————————————→			→	
Corporate		→————→			
Employees				→————————→	
Supervisors	→——→				

Note: Tail of arrow represents current attitude;
head of arrow represents desired attitude.

Figure 6-11 Charting Attitudes Toward the Design

Conducting the Sociotechnical Systems Analyses

- Identify resources to assist in the analyses
- Provide training in analytical methods
- Analyze system
- Review with steering committee
- Share with rest of organization

Figure 6-12 Conducting the Sociotechnical Systems Analyses

any event, cooperation from people at all levels of the organization will be required if valid data are to be obtained. If the system is complex, the design team may need to delegate parts of the analyses to others.

Provide training in analytical methods. The design team and others involved in conducting the analyses need detailed training in the analytical methods to be used. Given the importance of the analyses, taking time for thorough training is essential.

Analyze systems. The size and complexity of the organization along with the desired depth of the analyses determine the time needed to conduct them. Typically, the analyses require a total of two to four months to complete. Opportunities for immediate improvements in the organization may be discovered; if these opportunities do not conflict with the vision statement or require extensive resources to implement, they should be acted upon. Demonstrating incremental improvements can help to create or maintain support for the redesign process.

Review with the steering committee. The results of the analyses are reviewed with the steering committee in detail. The steering committee may wish only a summary report of the findings; but since redesign decisions will be based on the data, it is important for the steering committee to take the time necessary to understand the data fully. If the steering committee finds any of the data unclear or incomplete, the design team may have to undertake additional data gathering.

Share with rest of organization. Like the steering committee, organizational members need to understand the data in order to make sense of the changes proposed. Scheduling adequate time to review the data with the rest of the organization begins the process of transferring responsibility for the redesign from the design team to others.

Formulating Redesign Proposals

Formulating redesign proposals based on the analyses is the most important act the design team will perform. The steps illustrated in Figure 6-13 help to guide the selection of proposals.

Review design inputs. After spending time immersed in the process of data gathering, the design team should step back to review the expected outcomes of the redesign effort. The vision statement provides support for creative thinking about sweeping organizational changes and goals the redesign should achieve. The charter introduces minimum constraints upon the creative thinking proposed by the vision statement.

A review of sociotechnical systems theory and design principles helps to guide choices among possible alternatives. Learnings from visits to other organizations and from educational events provide tangible examples of how others have dealt with similar situations.

Formulate Redesign Proposals

- Review design inputs
- Clarify desired outcomes
- Formulate specific proposals
- Examine systemic impact
- Perform cost-benefit analysis
- Select most viable proposals
- Review with steering committee

Figure 6-13   Formulate Redesign Proposals

Then, reviewing the actual data collected helps identify areas where creative thinking can help to improve organizational effectiveness. At this point, brainstorming is more important than culling alternatives; decisions on which ideas to implement will be made later.

Clarify desired outcomes. As the design team generates ideas for improvement, it will become increasingly clear that more changes are possible than can be implemented. Clarifying the desired human and economic outcomes of the redesign will help to place the alternatives in perspective. Like shopping for a new car, the list of options becomes shorter as budget constraints are introduced; how much is eventually spent depends on what outcomes are desired and affordable. The vision statement serves as a preliminary statement of the outcomes; but discussion of the actual design alternatives will help to clarify the interests of various groups. During this phase, the tendency is to think conservatively; to adopt the simplest and cheapest changes; and to avoid disrupting operations if possible. How well these tendencies are resisted determines the actual potential for improvement in the redesign process.

Formulate specific proposals. Those alternatives which seem most promising are selected and given more detailed attention. How exactly would autonomous groups work here? How would their members be compensated? How would they be trained? How would they assess the performance of team members? How would leadership within the team be handled? What areas of responsibility should be given to the teams and when? Or, how should the technology be redesigned? What kind of inventory system should we adopt? How should we change the process to make it easier to control key variances? What additional technical training should be provided? What more information do people need to do a better job of controlling the technology? What should the roles of managers in this organization be?

Examine systemic impact. The major pieces of the redesign need to fit together like pieces of a jigsaw puzzle to form a coherent overall picture of the organization as a total system. Reward systems need to reinforce the new behaviors required to make the redesigned organization work; information systems need to get inventory to where it is needed on time; management systems need to work in harmony with the expectations of subordinates; technology needs to be designed to allow human control but not so as to create dull, repetitive jobs; governance systems need to incorporate opportunities for participation in policy making; hiring procedures need to take into account the new requirements for skills and membership; relationships with customers need to permit meaningful contact with employees; corporate policies need to be changed if necessary to allow the organization the freedom it needs to function in innovative ways; and so on. Every aspect of the design needs to be consistent with the values and intentions behind the effort, and mutually reinforcing in actual operation.

Perform cost-benefit analysis. To the extent possible, projections of implementation costs versus benefits should be prepared. These projections warn of possible excesses in the design as well as providing sound business reasons for implementing the suggested changes.

Select most viable proposals. Final proposals should move the organization toward the ideals expressed in the vision statement, meet any minimum constraints, fit with sociotechnical systems principles, work together smoothly, and appear economically viable.

Review with steering committee. Continuous communication between the design team and steering committee should make the discussion of proposals perfunctory rather than climactic. However, it is still important to ensure that the steering committee understands and accepts the proposals before communicating them publicly.

Implement Recommended Changes

As any experienced manager knows, good planning does not guarantee successful implementation. The gap between our intentions and reality defines the degree to which we meet our expectations for success. Two issues are fundamental to the transition between planning and implementation in sociotechnical systems redesign: (1) attaining the understanding and commitment of the entire organization to the changes proposed; and (2) developing a workable plan for overcoming organizational inertia. The procedures outlined in Figure 6-14 are intended to help close the planning-implementation gap.

Implement Recommended Changes

- Communicate and review proposals with rest of organization
- Communicate and review proposals with upper management
- Create implementation plan
- Train employees and supervisors
- Execute implementation plan

Figure 6-14 Implement Recommended Changes

Communicate and review proposals with the rest of the organization. To be understood and accepted, proposals for redesign need to be communicated first in such a way that organizational members who have not been intimately involved with the design team's work can grasp them. Individuals want to know what the proposed changes will mean to them on a day-to-day basis. The desire for detailed information suggests that large information meetings should be followed quickly by smaller group discussions or even one-on-one conversations with selected individuals.

Groups of employees with vested interests, such as more senior employees or those in the skilled trades, may balk at the idea of forming groups in which all members may eventually perform similar jobs. This resistance should have been anticipated and dealt with prior to the announcement of the final proposals but inevitably some resistance will remain. Since meeting each individual's concerns is unrealistic, the steering committee should consider whether or not they wish to allow individuals to remain in their previous roles in the redesigned system. If the number of individuals wishing to do so is small, forcing them to change may not be worth the cost; if many individuals feel this way, the design team needs to do further work on either the proposed changes or its implementation strategy.

Communicate and review proposals with upper management. Once the final proposals are clarified and found acceptable by organizational members, they should be discussed with upper management (corporate headquarters or its counterpart). Like the steering committee, upper management should have been kept informed throughout the redesign process, so that the review is anticlimactic. Where there is disagreement, a strong local champion may decide to defy his or her superiors; but the changes made in this way may not last once the champion leaves.

Create implementation plan. Sociotechnical systems redesign is complex, often requiring simultaneous changes in policies, reward systems, supervisory practices, contract provisions, relations with customers, work design, information systems, physical arrangements and technology. This amount of change is likely to be more than the organization has experienced during any time since its founding. The full benefit of the redesign will not become apparent until all of the changes are in place. Failure to change one aspect of the organization (reward systems, for example) may cancel out the effects of changing something else (like the introduction of more autonomous decision making).

Changes should be introduced from the outside-in; that is, large system changes (reward systems) should precede changes at the individual level (work design). The idea is to create the support and freedom needed for people to experiment successfully with new ways of working. To start from the core and work outwards would result in dissatisfaction as people find that policies and systems prevent them from taking advantage of opportunities to try out new behaviors. In reality, the change process will be messy; changes will be incremental rather than instantaneous; training will take time; and it will be found that some things can't be changed until the rest of the system is already functioning differently (quality control inspectors can't be eliminated until people learn how to inspect quality themselves, for example).

Having an implementation plan won't eliminate the confusion or incremental nature of change entirely; but it may ensure that important changes are not overlooked or unnecessarily delayed. Perhaps the most important function of the implementation plan is to assure people that changes in all aspects of the system are anticipated, even if they don't appear to be happening right away.

Train employees and supervisors. New systems require new skills. As mentioned before, training can begin prior to the implementation phase and continue indefinitely. As the details of the operation of the new system become clearer, additional needs for education may be identified.

Execute implementation plan. The design team's work isn't complete until the new system is functioning as it is supposed to. Like a project manager, the design team keeps the desired outcomes of the redesign process in perspective while adapting plans to meet current circumstances. Clearly, management must assume the responsibility for success of the implementation; but the design team can serve as a resource in overcoming difficulties without sacrificing the basic intentions of the design.

Evaluate Changes and Redesign

The two reasons for reconsidering changes that have been implemented are: (1) that the redesign has fallen short of desired outcomes; and (2) that internal or external changes have forced a rethinking of design decisions. In the first case, simple, one-time adjustments may be all that is called for; the latter requires that the organization possess an ongoing mechanism for sensing the fit between current operations and internal and external demands. Both of these are addressed in Figure 6-15.

Develop evaluation methodology. Conducting valid research is an art which, despite its years of practice in scientific circles, is still under development. Few managers or consultants have a taste for rigorous research; fortunately, most internal evaluations do not need to meet scholarly standards. Still, if not conducted properly, evaluations can produce misleading information that does more harm than good. Given all of the effort that went into redesign, it is sensible to make an investment in properly evaluating the effects of the changes over time.

The best approach is to involve a group of skilled, unbiased, external researchers in the follow up. These researchers can work closely with the design team in developing criteria for the success of the redesign, and then put together a valid approach for gathering data about the system. If the evaluation is done on a regular basis, trends can be detected which point toward the need for adjustments to the design.

Collect and review data against goals. The outcomes of the redesign are reviewed against the goals in the vision statement; in addition, it is important to consider the attitudes of employees and other stake-

Evaluate Changes and Redesign

- Develop evaluation methodology
- Collect and review data against goals
- Communicate results
- Redesign as needed
- Diffuse learnings

Figure 6-15   Evaluate Changes and Redesign

holders toward the new arrangements. Some data will be readily available from existing reports; special measures may need to be created to sense the climate of the new organization. When the data indicate a discrepancy with the intended outcomes, the steering committee has a choice: to change the vision statement or to change the system.

Redesign as needed. Because organizations are living systems, they are always changing—in both anticipated and unanticipated ways. Redesign is always occurring; the only question is whether or not it is intentional. Maintaining high performance requires intentional and continuous redesign as internal and external conditions change. Later redesigns can be dramatic, as when new technology is introduced; more often, they will be incremental and minor. In either case, the redesign process will be smoother if a design team of some kind continues in existence to assist with the transitions.

Diffuse learnings. Walton (1975) has argued that diffusion deserves special attention in redesign efforts. Diffusion prevents isolation and helps to institutionalize the changes that have been made. Walton noted that a high publicity approach to diffusion is unlikely to succeed, since other managers resent the attention given to the redesigned unit and feel resistant to changes forced upon them by the larger organization.

General Motors holds regular internal conferences to assist in the diffusion of learnings with the corporation (Landen & Carlson, 1982). Goodyear educates a group of line managers in organization development techniques each year and then returns them to line positions after they have had some experience acting as internal consultants.

Clearly, diffusion requires thoughtful planning and subtle approaches. Because the failure to diffuse an innovation can threaten its long-term viability, the work that follows a redesign effort can be as important and challenging as the redesign effort itself. While diffusion has become easier as sociotechnical systems innovation has become more popular, it is still an area in which we have much to learn.

Summary

The model presented in this chapter is an overview of one approach to sociotechnical systems redesign. It is not the only one; nor is it likely to be appropriate in every organization. Following any model dogmatically usually produces disappointment as outcomes fall short of those desired. A model like this one can be helpful, but following it should not be the goal; the goal is to get there as easily and effectively as possible. It's often a good sign when managers toss models aside and say, "This process isn't right for us—let's design one that is." More often than not, they're right—and they can—and it works.

CHAPTER SEVEN

Leadership in Sociotechnical Systems

Despite the important role that leaders play in supporting sociotechnical systems experimentation, the issue of leadership has only recently begun to be discussed. Much of the research done in this area has been motivated by the fact that it is often managers, not employees, who offer the greatest resistance to sociotechnical systems redesign (Bushe, 1983; Walton & Schlesinger, 1979). This isn't surprising when one considers that some sociotechnically designed organizations, like Digital Equipment's Enfield plant, operate with no first line supervisors and very few managers overall. Even when their job security isn't threatened by sociotechnical systems redesign, managers still face the challenge of defining new roles for themselves at a time when employees are striving for maximum autonomy. This chapter examines why the role of leaders is changing, and what some aspects of their new role might be.

Forces Affecting the Twenty-first Century Leader

The environment is becoming increasingly complex at the same time that organizations are becoming more sensitive to it; new designs for work and organization are required if organizations are to be effective in the future. Some time ago, Bennis (1966) declared that the bureaucratic model was no longer suited to our time, given rapid and unexpected changes in the environment, growth in organizational complexity, increased diversity and specialization among organizational members and changes in managerial beliefs which embrace more humanistic assumptions about the nature of man.

Clearly, the trends noted by Bennis have not abated. New tools, based on quantum microelectronics, information theory, laser technology, biomechanical engineering and astrophysics have brought new waves of specialists into organizations, each with their own knowledge base and distinctive language. Electronic information processing has tightened the link between the organization and its environment. Computers allow more information to be used in decision making so that authority based upon position is giving way to authority based on information. The economy is evolving from routine, predictable manufacturing employment to nonroutine, adaptive service employment. Government, in its concern for the ecology and the welfare of the people, is regulating more industries in more impactful ways. Families are less a stabilizing force in our lives; and while we are less connected to one another at home, we are globally more interconnected than ever before.

Toffler (1980) has summarized the impacts of these trends on organizations of the future as follows:

Earlier we saw that when all the second wave principles were put to work in a single organization the result was a classical industrial bureaucracy; a giant, hierarchical, permanent, top-down, mechanistic organization, well designed for making repetitive products or repetitive decisions in a comparatively stable industrial environment. Now, however, as we shift to the new principles and begin to apply them together, we are necessarily led to wholly new kinds of organizations for the future. These third wave organizations have flatter hierarchies. They are less top-heavy. They consist of small components linked together in temporary configurations ... they are what might be called "dual" or "poly" organizations, capable of assuming two or more distinct structural shapes as conditions warrant—rather like some plastic of the future which will change shape when heat or cold is applied but spring back into a basic form when the temperature is in the normal range (p. 263).

About managers of the future, Toffler says:

We need managers who can operate as capably in an open-door, free-flow style as in a hierarchical mode, who can work in an organization structured like an Egyptian pyramid as well as one that looks like a Calder mobile, with a few of their managerial strands holding a complex set of nearly autonomous modules that move in response to the gentlest breeze (p. 264).

Thus, the organizations in which leaders will manage are changing; but so are the leaders themselves. Leaders of today are better educated than leaders of twenty years ago. Despite well-founded concerns about the nature of collegiate business education (Fry & Pasmore, 1983), the fact is that more managers are beginning their careers or advancing them with more years of formal education. According to a report by *Time Magazine* (May 4, 1981), colleges granted only 4,643 MBA degrees in 1960; by 1970 the number had grown to 21,599 and in 1981 more than 54,000 managers received MBAs. Currently, more than half a million managers hold MBAs, and the trend is not slacking off.

If anything, the trend will be toward additional education; given the increasingly sophisticated technology of the 21st century, it is likely that managers will take technical training to complement their business skills. Much of this training is currently being provided by organizations and it is probable that organizations will increase the amount they spend on technical training for managers in the future.

In addition to educational changes, there are demographic changes occurring among leaders as well. The roles of women and minorities continue to evolve in ways that afford these groups more equal opportunity to assume leadership positions. Organizations are becoming less dominated by white males and more multicultural in their leadership and climate (Kanter, 1977).

Among leaders in general, there is a trend toward being more sensitive to human as well as economic objectives. The increase in the number of organizations engaging in organization development activities is an indication that over two decades after McGregor (1960), theory Y values about people are gradually beginning to take hold.

Hence, organizations and those who lead them are becoming increasingly complex and more capable of doing more things. These added capacities come none too soon, as organizations are being more intensively pressured by their environment to pay attention to a broad range of economic and social demands. Leaders of the future will be less able to operate their organizations as if in vacuums, pleading ignorance as an excuse for damaging the social or biological ecosphere. Already, there is clear evidence of the increased time managers must spend on dealing with legal issues confronting their firms (Pfeffer & Salancik, 1978).

The leader of the future will need to be more comfortable with the uncertainty created by changes inside and outside of the organization. He or she will need to help others make sense out of seemingly disassociated events or signals, motivating others and transforming their views of reality in the process (Weick, 1979). He or she will spend more time managing change and less time managing the status quo. Furthermore, increased technical sophistication and accompanying specialization will force leaders to pay more attention to their role as integrators if the actions of specialists are to be coordinated effectively (Lawrence & Lorsch, 1967).

Finally, leaders of all organizations will continue to be influenced by research which demonstrates that organizational effectiveness can be increased by allowing more complete employee involvement in decision making. The role of the leader as hero or heroine is giving way to the role of leader as team captain or even first among equals.

The forces shown in Figure 7-1 would seem to call for new leadership behaviors and new organization designs; yet there are still far fewer sociotechnically designed organizations than there are traditional bureaucracies with traditional leaders. Why?

Some authors remain steadfast in the belief that bureaucracy is the optimal organizational form (Perrow, 1972; Miewald, 1970; Robbins, 1983). These authors argue that bureaucracy works; that they have grown to large sizes successfully; that core societal values are changing only slowly; that environmental turbulence is exaggerated; that professionalization has replaced position power without changing the basic nature of bureaucracy; and that leaders will continue to prefer the control afforded them by bureaucratic structures.

Despite four decades of research and application since Maslow first published his theory on the motivational needs of man (1943); three decades of research and experimentation following Trist and Bamforth's report on the impact of sociotechnical systems arrangements on the productivity and behavior of coal miners (1951); and over two decades of promoting theory Y values among managers, there still remain two competing views of how to control behavior in organizations.

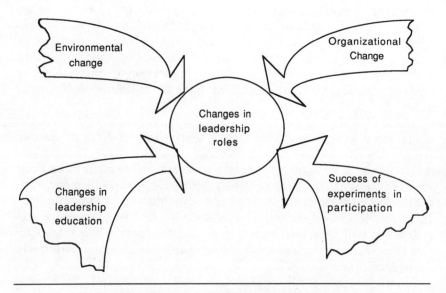

Figure 7-1 Forces Affecting Leadership Roles

The first view is based on the belief that people must be coerced into working in organizations because they would not choose to do so of their own free will (Etzioni, 1963; Galbraith, 1977). The second view is based on the belief that organizations provide the means for identity development, personal growth and self-actualization and therefore that people will be intrinsically motivated to perform the tasks requested of them. The first view leads to strategies of domination, control and bureaucratization; the second to strategies which emphasize mutual learning, participative decision making, concern for human needs and adhocracy (Bennis, 1966).

Which view is correct? Both and neither. There are clearly some jobs in organizations which surpass the normal limits of human indifference and for which extrinsic rewards or coercion are required to motivate people to perform them (Barnard, 1938). Moreover, it is difficult to imagine a large organization performing a prescribed repetitive function (the post office, for example) that would not operate in a bureaucratic manner.

At the same time, there is evidence that views of human nature produce self-fulfilling prophecies (Argyris, 1964; Rosenthal & Jacobson, 1968; Eden, 1988). When treated like adults and given responsibility, people act responsibly. When treated with mistrust, people often act in untrustworthy, irresponsible ways. Hence, managers who work in organizations designed to control untrustworthy employees will find ample data that the structures they work in are necessary, while managers who work in organizations designed for mature adults will experience quite different behaviors.

While not denying the appropriateness of bureaucratic control for some situations, it seems that too often leaders make the mistake of creating self-fulfilling prophecies by designing organizations based on theory X beliefs. They do so because they are more familiar with bureaucratic organizational models, because they enjoy the power they experience in such organizations and feel comfortable with the sense that their leadership will not be questioned (Hackman, 1978). Their organizations continue to persist (in some cases) in spite of rapidly changing environmental demands because they are only loosely-coupled with the environment, so that changes don't affect them immediately or directly (Weick, 1979). Given the imperfect nature of most competition, organizations are able to accumulate and utilize slack resources despite their lack of fit with their internal and external environments (Galbraith, 1977). Hence, it is appropriate to conclude that the majority of organizations designed upon theory X beliefs will survive for a while longer, but do so only by operating at a level below their maximum effectiveness.

If, on the other hand, leaders agree that innovation is called for, they will face uncertainty, disbelief and challenges on all fronts. Often, even the people they are trying to help will resist their suggestions, because they view the unhappy status quo as more attractive than an uncertain future (Morris, 1987). If they do decide to innovate, leaders can expect their own roles to change dramatically. What will some of these changes be?

The Role of the Leader in Sociotechnical Systems

In a study of over 60 work groups involved in quality of work life projects in seven organizations, Trist and Dwyer (1982) found that managers had allowed almost all of the projects to die out despite the impressive results that had been achieved. In many of the projects, employees perceived their supervisors as not just disinterested, but negative toward the quality of work life activities. The reason for this was that managers felt caught in a bind:

> Two sets of objectives that could not be satisfied simultaneously were being communicated to them from their superiors: (1) get the work groups functioning; (2) maintain performance levels. . . . Several foremen felt that they were receiving neither the moral nor the resource support to address effectively this new set of demands. Moral support-interest and involvement in the functioning of the groups did not come from their superiors; and resource support did not come from equipment, maintenance, personnel, supplies of materials to the groups, or plant planners (p.177).

Furthermore, those interviewed felt that as one went up the management ladder, the clarity of support diminished. In retrospect, participants stated emphatically that management's attitude toward quality of work life should have been more thoroughly addressed before change was embarked upon. Management was perceived as: unwilling to change roles or policies that inhibited the more autonomous functioning of groups; slow to respond to suggestions; not directly involved enough in monitoring the process and helping to solve problems; unclear on their roles in the new system; insufficiently communicative with other groups; poorly trained in group process facilitation and conflict management; frightened by the support of the union for the process; and generally "going along with the program" instead of actively trying to make it work.

When Trist and Dwyer shared these data with the corporate mangers involved, their response was the following:

> Most of those present were inclined to accept these views at least to some degree. Work involvement through QWL was indeed a long-range strategic undertaking requiring a large investment of management time and energy

and a large investment in the training and development of the work force as well as those in supervisory and plant-management ranks. This was a daunting prospect. The company, some of those present pointed out, had other formidable priorities in the technological field regarding new products and manufacturing processes. The changes entailed would strain the capacities of operational managers for the foreseeable future. These managers could not be asked to undertake a major parallel task, expecially as their views on QWL were contradictory. Our systems of management practice, they said, had stood the test of time and in labor relations, at least, both sides knew where they stood (p.179).

Like many other organizations of our times, this one was apparently preparing to charge headlong into the future while facing squarely backwards. Similar information on the difficulties managers have in adjusting to organizations undergoing sociotechnical systems transformations is provided by Walton and Schlesinger (1979) in a study of twelve companies. Among the problems they observed were such things as neglecting distinctions between start-up and steady state operations, unrealistic expectations, and lack of adequate support.

Added to these difficulties is the lack of role clarity for managers that accompanies the transition from traditional to high performance work systems. As workers become members of autonomous groups, the role of foreman changes from that of director to coordinator or technical expert, with a focus on training, problem solving, providing resources, counselling, negotiating, linking, sharing information, and managing continuous change. Middle managers, who used to perform many of these functions, would then be free to concentrate on technical development, general planning and interrelationships among departments. Top managers would focus on strategic planning, policy, management development and the relation of the company to the environment.

Mans and Sims (1983) likewise view the role of the foreman as changing from that of director to coordinator; in fact, they label the holder of this new role as "the unleader" because his or her activities are so different from those of traditional supervisors. They separate the new behaviors required into two categories: those dealing with behavior within the work group and those dealing with managing the boundary between the work group and its environment.

Within-group responsibilities include encouraging the group to communicate, plan, make its own work assignments, reinforce each other for high performance, set goals, be self-observant, provide feedback to one another, and think through activities before performing them. Boundary management tasks include communicating to and from management, linking different work groups, helping to train inexperienced employees, facilitating the availability of equipment and supplies, facilitating the flow of production between groups, and communicating with other leaders of groups.

Lippit (1982) cited six trends which he believed would greatly affect the roles of leaders: the double bind of maintaining quality with reduced resources; expectations of shared responsibility; interdependence; more people needed for problem solving; the integration of human and technical systems; and the need for new competencies. Lippit believed that in order to respond successfully to these challenges, leaders must abandon their socialized values regarding the sanctity of vertical authority, become more comfortable with people at lower levels assuming responsibility for tasks, feel more comfortable with interdependence versus independence, give up the idea that competition is necessary for achievement, and instead promote mutual support, the sharing of resources and the pooling of complimentary abilities. In addition, he felt that leaders would need to be open to alternatives for reallocating scarce resources, be more resourceful in finding innovative ways to do more with less, become more comfortable with relying on others for support while finding the courage in themselves to take risks, achieve a balance of focus on task and people, develop means to bring together people of diverse viewpoints and backgrounds and molding them into teams, and be more open to working collaboratively with outside groups.

Schlesinger (1983) pays specific attention to the role of the middle manager in sociotechnically designed organizations. Because lower level managers frequently assume middle management responsibilities after their groups begin to fulfill first line management duties themselves, middle managers sometimes find themselves being squeezed out of meaningful roles. They find that top management is not willing to give up its traditional role in strategic planning or in managing environmental relationships, so they find themselves being left with vaguely defined coordinative responsibilities. Schlesinger recommends the formation of coalitions of middle managers to afford them the power to shape roles for themselves as integrators and developers of others, or whatever other roles fit the needs of the organizations they belong to.

Some activities middle managers might devote themselves to are described by Yukl (1981):

Developing better relationships with superiors to increase trust in lower level managers and workers for solving their own problems.

Gaining more control over input acquisition and output disposal by developing relationships with suppliers and customers and seeking alternative sources and outlets.

Initiating new activities, products or services to make better use of existing resources.

Changing the organization or work unit structure to solve chronic problems and reduce the need for disturbance-handling activities.

In summary, it would appear that the roles of leaders in sociotechnically designed organizations will be more complex and varied than those in traditionally designed organizations. The new roles will include being facilitators, process consultants, liaisons, linking pins, integrators, innovators, decision makers, evaluators, network builders, conflict managers, resource allocators and inspirationalists. Descriptions of these roles are provided in Figure 7-2.

Will managers be able to adjust to these new roles? Klein and Posey (1986) offer the observation that the managers who have been the most successful in traditional systems should have no trouble adapting to their roles in innovative systems. In their study of a traditional and innovative organization, Klein and Posey found that successful managers in both exhibited the same characteristics: they are competent, caring, and committed to both the work and their people; they emphasize quality, provide clear direction, and motivate with accurate and timely feedback; they coach their workers and share information; they take responsibility for outcomes, know how to get the right people involved in problem solving and do so; and they look beyond their own areas to understand the plant and company as a whole.

Thus, it would appear that competent managers have no cause for concern regarding their roles in innovative work systems; the future for them is more of the same. But for others who depend on the support provided by traditional hierarchical systems, the move to a sociotechnically designed organization could be a shock. For them, additional training, coaching and counselling may be necessary.

Summary

The environment is demanding changes in organizations, and leaders are not immune. Organizations of the future will not be manageable by current methods; but the best of today's managers should find no discomfort in transitioning to roles in new organizational systems.

Leaders, like navigators of ships, need to understand both their own positions and the directions they must take to arrive at desired destinations. Unfortunately, neither can be calculated using objective instruments. Unlike the sea, the stars and the continents, organizations are intangible social arrangements. Positions vary depending upon the observer's frame of reference; directions are frequently unknown; and

1. Facilitators/Process Consultants: managers will need to facilitate the flow of information in groups and between groups. Part of this role means understanding what is happening from a more holistic point of view. The manager in this role, in addition to attention paid to content, will need to pay close attention to process - the way people work together to accomplish objectives.

2. Liasons/Linking Pins/Network Builders: formally or informally, managers will be in a position to bring groups together to solve common problems. Work within groups is constantly affected by actions of external groups with whom the leader should relate.

3. Integrator/Innovator/Decision Maker: managers must be able to integrate information, conceptualize possible alternatives, and plan productive courses of action. Moreover, they must approach problem solving in innovative and participative ways.

4. Conflict Managers/Relationship Builders: as the number of parties involved in problem solving increases, so does the number of different points of view. Leaders need to develop skills to manage conflict productively and build cooperative relationships among interdependent groups.

5. Evaluators/Resource Allocators: these roles are traditional, but become even more important in sociotechnically designed organizations. Helping employees learn to evaluate their own and one another's performance takes time and patience; allocating resources also becomes more challenging when leaders can no longer rely on hierarchical authority to make resource allocation decisions.

6. Inspirational Leader: leaders will need to help maintain a common vision among different autonomous groups. Leaders will also have to push for exploration of what is possible rather than relying on rules to point the way toward the future.

Figure 7-2 New Roles for Leaders in Sociotechnical Systems

even destinations are under continuous debate. To set a route and stick to it in this context requires awareness of social winds, political reefs, technological tides, economic maelstroms and consensually validated charts. The navigator of a human ship can never know the distance to port, because the voyage is never complete until the ship can no longer sail. The leader is no more or less than a manager of transitions.

CHAPTER EIGHT

Sociotechnical Systems: Where from Here?

The preceding chapters have addressed the sociotechnical systems approach as it has evolved over the past four decades. At this point, it seems appropriate to speculate on the future, with particular attention to forces that may make our current thinking about sociotechnical systems design obsolete.

Values

While the methods we use to diagnose and intervene in systems may change in the next 50 years, the values that underlie the sociotechnical systems paradigm probably will not. Values change more slowly than the techniques we will find acceptable as additions to our general approach. The values which I believe will remain central features of the sociotechnical systems tradition are described in the following paragraphs.

Ownership and commitment through participation. We believe strongly that people should have a say in shaping their destinies, both in and outside of the workplace. At a pragmatic level, we know from Lewin's early studies (1948, 1958) that participation leads to the acceptance of decisions; effective behavioral change follows meaningful involvement in decision making. People understand the decisions they make more fully, are more aware of the forces that drive the decision, are more likely to have considered potential barriers to implementing the decision, and often are more likely to be supported by others in making the decision work. Peoples' needs are more likely to be taken into account in participative decision making; and as a result they are more likely to feel that they are being treated like responsible, intelligent adults who are capable of self-directed activity toward goals that are mutually acceptable and inherently rewarding. Participative decisions are therefore less likely to produce alienation, dissatisfaction or the withholding of cooperation (Kanter, 1983).

Beyond the obvious benefits of participation, we value the right of people to be free, that is, to affect governance decisions that may impact the quality of their lives. While democracy and participation are not necessarily synonomous (democracy implies one person-one vote, while participation simply means involvement), few would argue that the concepts are incompatible. To the extent that we recognize every individual's right to choose where he or she lives and how he or she earns a living, we are promoting democracy. Eventually, the growing workplace democracy movement (Simmons & Mares, 1983) may change the nature of relationships between the majority of employees and their organizations. More employees can be expected to become part-owners of the organizations they work for, and even those who don't will demand greater influence in all kinds of decisions that affect their future livelihood.

Sociotechnical systems theory holds that variances should be controlled at their source; the continuing push for greater participation will fight against arbitrary constraints that interfere with responsible problem solving and autonomous variance control. Organizations work best when people are allowed to do everything within their power to help the organization succeed. Participation, both broad and deep, will continue to be a primary feature of sociotechnical systems design.

Developing people. We value the continued growth of people through life-long learning. We believe that there is no limit to what people can learn; and that more capable people will use their enhanced knowledge to improve organizational effectiveness. Learning makes working worthwhile; it enriches one's self-esteem as well as one's ability to perform more proficiently. Continuous learning helps us to avoid rigidity in our thinking and boredom in our routines; it exposes us to the worlds of others, so that we can work together more effectively; it opens up new career possibilities; helps us to reconceptualize old problems in order to seek new solutions; enhances our creativity and self-confidence; and helps us to relate to one another in a different manner and context than we are accustomed to.

Learning may be forgotten or underutilized; still, we value it. Learning does not translate directly or immediately into bottom line performance improvements, but we know that it does eventually. We are aware of our own learning and how valuable it has been to our own success; and we are sometimes shocked to see how much we still need to learn when we undertake tasks in a new arena.

What we need to learn is always changing as the world around us changes; and as open systems, organizations are always importing new learners or creating new learning situations for those who have already learned once but need to relearn again. Sociotechnical systems designers will continue to value learning, and seek even better ways to reinforce its occurrence through organizational redesign.

Making technology more compassionate. As noted earlier, few sociotechnical systems efforts have actually involved technological redesign. The worlds of technical experts and social scientists are still too far apart for the work of one group to inform the work of the other.

In retrospect, we see the jobs created during the industrial revolution to be needlessly demeaning and in fact suboptimal in terms of the performance results they produced. Yet we have not learned from our past experience how to design technology which is more compassionate in terms of its effects on people. Indeed, the computer-aided high tech revolution is repeating several negative aspects of the industrial revolution: job displacement; monotonous, unchallenging jobs; extreme faith in technical solutions to competitive problems; the creation of a technological elite who control decision making; and capital diversion from alternative improvement possibilities.

We value competitiveness and technological advancement. I am certainly not advocating a "no further technological progress" doctrine. However, I think that we also must value the quality of working life more highly than we once did. We noticed a surge of interest in the quality of life during the 1970s, and a recession of concern in the 1980s. This was due, in part, to the fact that many of the programs in the 1970s had a mistaken notion of what improving the quality of work life meant. For almost everyone involved, the focus was more on making people happy or getting them involved than it was on making them truly productive. While they were treated differently, most people did not experience a dramatic change in how they went about doing their work from day to day or a leap in the quality of their working lives.

The sociotechnical systems approach views the same objective of improving the quality of work life quite differently. In the sociotechnical systems perspective, the way to enhance quality of work life is to change what people actually do at work, and in ways that make them more productive, more able to use their knowledge and skills, more able to cooperate with others in solving interdependent problems, more able to expand their capabilities, more autonomous in their control, more in charge of the technology they operate and more secure about their future.

Hopefully, most people will be more satisfied and involved once these changes have been introduced; but making people happy or involving them in problem-solving discussions for an hour a week is not what sociotechnical systems design is all about.

Well-designed work produces higher levels of commitment and performance than poorly-designed work. To the extent that technology influences the design of work, we need to influence the design of technology in order to affect the performance of organizations.

Sharing rewards. We believe that hard work should be rewarded fairly. We fight against the oppression of the poor by greedy businessmen who offer only the choice between low-paying work and no work at all. We extend this basic value to include sharing gains obtained through the contribution of ideas. If an organization is made more profitable through the hard work and creative thinking of its members, it seems fair that those members should share in the financial results. Of course, the immediate sharing of rewards must be balanced against investment in a more secure future; but I believe that people who are able to generate enhanced profits are able to make informed, intelligent decisions about the best way to use those profits.

We know from observing entrepreneurs that many people are capable of running their own businesses in a financially responsible manner. We are also witness to the tremendous energies entrepreneurs put forth in exchange for what appear to be relatively small financial rewards. The links between motivation, decision making, ownership, profit sharing and the opportunity to determine one's future are well documented. For moral as well as economic reasons, sociotechnical systems designers will continue to value arrangements which permit the fruits of labor to be shared with those who help to grow them.

Becoming more comfortable with change. Sociotechnical systems designers would make poor artists because they would never finish the pieces that they started. Designers value incompletion, because they recognize that the environment will make any design obsolete eventually. Most of us value stability in our lives; it is comforting to know what can be expected in the future, so that we can plan accordingly. But sociotechnical systems designers place value in becoming more comfortable with change as a continuous part of life. Small changes are less wrenching and easier to make than large ones; and if change is inevitable, better that it be recognized as such and dealt with accordingly.

In any system that is seemingly unchanging at first glance, dynamic forces are at work that will eventually produce change. In organizations, people age, as does technology; knowledge grows; materials are used up and new ones are developed; information becomes available; problems develop; the market shifts directions; profits rise or fall; disagreements occur; and experience accumulates. Changes are incessant as a consequence of this ongoing turbulence; but this does not mean that the organization is out of control. It simply means that the organization will be more effective if it can develop better control mechanisms to help it adapt to change in productive rather than regressive ways.

Therefore, sociotechnical systems designers view change as an ally, as something which yields clues to ways to make the organization more effective. Processes which involve people in recognizing change and controlling responses to it will continue to be valued as a part of sociotechnical systems design.

Reaching out versus closing in. We are attracted to issues which are clear, near to us and which we feel that we can control. We are less attracted to unstructured problems which seem distant and beyond our influence (March & Simon, 1958). What happens outside of an organization is often more like the latter than the former; it is difficult to know what is happening to begin with, let alone what can be done in response. Yet sociotechnical systems designers know that the future of organizations will be determined as much if not more by external events than internal ones, and so value staying in touch with the outside world and being proactive in shaping external events.

Given a choice, sociotechnical systems designers would prefer to see those near the top of an organization spending more time dealing with external issues than internal ones. Designers would also like to see ways developed for every organizational member to spend at least some time in touch with some element of the environment. There will always be more internal problems and opportunities to deal with than time allows; so only a clearly stated value that internal concerns should not drive out attention to the external environment can prevent myopia from setting in and threatening the ability of the organization to adapt to its changing habitat.

Cooperation versus competition. Sometimes it seems that organizations have been designed intentionally to ensure that people who should work together on a task cannot. Departmental boundaries, hierarchical levels, job classifications, individual reward systems, restricted communication and politics create barriers to effective teamwork. Yet organizations exist to accomplish tasks that individuals could not perform by working alone; so one must ask why such a gap exists between intention and reality.

Sociotechnical systems designers value cooperation over unhealthy conflict. Unhealthy conflict arises when goals differ and personal gains associated with independent actions outweigh the benefits of collective action (Sherif, 1966). Conflict can be healthy if it produces enhanced alternatives to problem solving and if a foundation of trust underlies superficial disagreements. But conflict can be destructive if it creates win-lose dynamics (Walton, 1987).

Because individual concerns find their way into organizations easily and can destroy cooperation, Weber (1947) suggested bureaucracy as a means of separating individual and organizational interests. Bureaucracy has proven a poor solution to this problem, however, as the power of bureaucracies continues to be subverted to meet individual goals (Perrow, 1972).

Instead, sociotechnical systems designers seek to enhance the rewards for achieving superordinate goals while simultaneously abolishing barriers to cooperation. The idea is not to separate individuals from the offices they hold, but to make the health of the whole more important than the well-being of the parts, and also to make office-holding a collective versus individual responsibility.

Valuing cooperation over competition also means supporting interpersonal skill training, process consultation, open communication, abundant information, reducing hierarchical levels, frequent meetings, sharing knowledge and striving for equal treatment.

The ultimate value. Although it appears self-evident, sociotechnical systems designers value striving for high performance. Satisficing (March & Simon, 1958) is not likely to produce conditions which bring out the best in people or which provide them with high quality of work life. Striving for high performance means investing in the future, developing people, being open to new ideas and making them work, recognizing opportunities for improvement and acting upon them, being proud of what has been accomplished but always trying to do better, learning more than is already known, caring about the long-term impacts of short-term decisions, helping out peers versus striving for individual stardom, utilizing machines and materials wisely, being more aware of the external environment and, in fact, caring about what this book is all about.

Valuing high performance does not mean cutting costs just to look good this quarter, hiring cheap labor, opting not to do preventive maintenance, building departmental empires, reviewing every decision that has been made, punishing mistakes, ignoring the competition, alienating customers, working with outdated technology, trying to do more than can be done well, assuming that problems will go away if they are left alone, maintaining distance between management and labor, holding onto the past despite obvious signs that the present is different, and not trying to improve.

Valuing high performance requires systemic thinking; thinking about the social system as well as the technical system and about the external as well as the internal environment. Designing an effective organization using the sociotechnical systems approach is a deliberate and choiceful act, based on idealistic values.

Some Possible Changes in the Sociotechnical Systems Paradigm

Given the stability of the values just outlined, it's unlikely that the sociotechnical systems paradigm will experience major upheavals in the future. More probably, changes will occur in where and how the fundamental ideas are applied.

New applications for sociotechnical systems thinking. With the shift in our economy from manufacturing to service work, sociotechnical systems thinking needs to further refine its ideas regarding the analysis and design of work in non-routine settings. Pava (1983, 1987) has contributed important ideas in this regard, but the evolution of thought on this front needs to continue. Although much work in service settings is routine and can be thought of using the existing sociotechnical systems paradigm, much more work is becoming non-routine and unanalyzable by traditional methods.

Applications of new methods for analyzing non-routine systems are still spotty and results mixed; yet the need to develop sociotechnical thinking to help transform these enivronments is urgent. Health care organizations, for example, are buckling under severe pressure from the government and consumers to reduce the costs of patient care; yet there have been few sociotechnical systems applications in health care organizations and the results of those have not been uniformly positive (Chisholm & Ziegenfuss, 1987; Pasmore, Petee & Bastian, 1987).

Other settings in need of intensive care include research and development organizations; government; universities; small businesses and family firms; schools; mental health institutions; the military; insurance companies; financial institutions; and the staff and managerial portions of most major corporations. Beyond our own borders, there is much work to be done in applying sociotechnical systems thinking in developing countries (Kiggundu, 1987) and perhaps even in the exploration of outer space (Schoonhoven, 1987). The opportunities for new applications are rich and varied.

Changes in how sociotechnical systems thinking is applied. In addition to new sites for sociotechnical systems applications, there will also undoubtedly be changes in how sociotechnical systems methods are applied. These range from considering sociotechnical systems design as a national policy, as in Norway (Elden, 1987); as a community development activity, as in the case of Jamestown, New York (Trist, 1987); or as a way to deal with the effective integration of new technologies (Susman & Chase, 1987). Whenever there are people, working together in a system with technology, in an environment that provides resources the system needs, there is the possibility of adapting sociotechnical systems thinking to help improve the system's effectiveness. The scope of the system, its complexity and its objectives don't matter; the theory is robust and powerful.

Conclusion

Every organization is a sociotechnical system. Not every organization is designed using sociotechnical systems principles and methods. Organizations are not immutable; their members can choose to change them if they desire. I hope that this book has made this point clearly, and that it motivates those who read it to challenge themselves to act accordingly.

APPENDIX A

STS ASSESSMENT SURVEY
(STSAS)

Introduction: This instrument is intended for use in assessing organizations to determine the extent to which their designs are consistent with sociotechnical systems (STS) principles, which have been demonstrated to produce high levels of commitment and performance. The STSAS may be administered to an entire organization or to subunits. It may be used prior to a sociotechnical systems intervention to guide organizational improvement; or during or after an intervention to assess progress in designing the organization for high performance.

William A. Pasmore, Ph.D.
Department of Organizational Behavior
Weatherhead School of Management
Case Western Reserve University
Cleveland, Ohio 44106
(216) 368-2138

Dimensions: The STSAS measures six dimensions of sociotechnical systems design, defined as follows:

Innovativeness: The extent to which organizational leaders and members maintain a futuristic versus historical orientation; their propensity for risk taking; rewards for innovation.

Human Resource Development The extent to which the talents, knowledge, skills and ability of organizational members are developed and tapped; work design; supervisory roles; organizational structure; workflow structure.

157

Environmental Agility: The extent to which the organization maintains awareness of the environment and responds appropriately to it; customer importance; proactivity vs. reactivity; structural flexibility; technical flexibility; product/service flexibility.

Cooperation: The extent to which individuals and subunits work together to accomplish superordinate goals; teamwork; mutual support; shared values; common rewards.

Commitment/Energy: The extent to which organizational members are dedicated to accomplishing organizational goals and are prepared to expend energy in doing so; reward systems; information availability.

Joint Optimization: The extent to which the organization is designed to use both its social and technical resources effectively; variance control; the appropriateness of technology; the extent to which technology is designed to support teamwork, flexibility and changes in organizational structure.

Instructions: Each dimension of STS design is measured by several questions. Since organizations are unique in terms of their history, goals, social systems, technical systems and environments, not all questions will apply to every organization; nor will the high end of each scale be ideal in every instance. Generally speaking, however, the closer the organization is to the high end of each question ("5" on the five-point scale) the more it conforms to STS design principles.

Respondents should read the descriptions of the endpoints and midpoint for each question and then circle a number from 1 to 5 which most closely approximates their view of their organization or unit. For example, the "2" circled in the question below would indicate that the person completing the survey felt that his/her boss shared some, but a relatively small amount of information concerning the state of the business:

Sample
Question:

| 1 | 2 | 3 | 4 | 5 |

My boss never shares any information about the state of the business with me

My boss shares some information about the business with me, but not on a regular basis

My boss shares a great deal of information about the business with me in regularly scheduled meetings for this purpose

Once all questions have been completed, respondents may choose to transfer their scores for each question to the summary sheet at the end of the survey in order to view the overall pattern of scores.

INNOVATIVENESS

Time Orientation

Question 1

| 1 | 2 | 3 | 4 | 5 |

Management is more concerned with preserving the status quo than with what is happening now or what will happen in the future

Management is more concerned with what happens today than what happened yesterday or will happen tomorrow

Management is more concerned about the future than it is with what is happening today or what has happened in the past

Question 2

| 1 | 2 | 3 | 4 | 5 |

Most people here are concerned about security; they resist change

Some people here are open to change if it is absolutely necessary and not too disruptive

Most people here welcome change and view it as healthy and non-threatening

159

Question 3

1	2	3	4	5
New ideas are ignored; the motto is, "Don't fix it if it's not broken"		New ideas are sometimes listened to		New ideas are constantly sought and tried

Question 4

1	2	3	4	5
Past mistakes are never forgiven		Past mistakes are sometimes forgiven		Past mistakes are forgiven; the focus is on how to do it better

Risk Taking

Question 5

1	2	3	4	5
Most people here are afraid to take risks		Some people here take some risks, but not big ones		Most people here are not afraid to take risks, especially when they are important

Question 6

1	2	3	4	5
When people take a risk here, they do it alone		When people take a risk here, they are supported by a few others		There is widespread support for risk taking here

Question 7

1	2	3	4	5
People who take risks and fail are punished		People who take risks and fail are not punished, but are told not to try again		People who take risks and fail are not punished and are told to try again

Rewards for Innovation

Question 8

People who help make changes are seldom recognized for their efforts

1 ─

2 ─

People who make changes are sometimes recognized for their efforts

3 ─

4 ─

People who help make changes are frequently recognized for their efforts

5 ─

Question 9

New ideas are viewed as bothersome and are not rewarded

1 ─

2 ─

New ideas are neither encouraged nor discouraged; token rewards are sometimes offered

3 ─

4 ─

New ideas are sought and rewarded in a meaningful way

5 ─

Question 10

People who try to change things here are not promoted

1 ─

2 ─

People who try to change things here are sometimes promoted

3 ─

4 ─

People who try to change things here are usually promoted

5 ─

HUMAN RESOURCES DEVELOPMENT/UTILIZATION

Opportunities for Learning

Question 11

There are few opportunities here for people to learn new skills or knowledge

1 ─

2 ─

There are some opportunities to learn, but few people take advantage of them

3 ─

4 ─

There are many opportunities for people to learn new skills or knowledge and most people take advantage of them

5 ─

Question 12

People have a lot of potential for growth that hasn't been tapped here

1 —

2 —

People have grown here, but not as much as I would have liked

3 —

4 —

People feel like they're working to their full potential here; they have grown a lot

5 —

Question 13

This organization makes it difficult to acquire the skills you need to progress

1 —

2 —

This organization provides some help in getting the skills you need to progress

3 —

4 —

This organization makes it easy to get the skills you need to progress

5 —

Question 14

There are no rewards for learning here

1 —

2 —

There are few rewards for learning here

3 —

4 —

Learning is well-rewarded here

5 —

Question 15

It's difficult to learn much outside of the scope of one's own job

1 —

2 —

People are allowed to learn a few things outside the scope of their job

3 —

4 —

People are encouraged to learn as much as they can about all aspects of the organization

5 —

Question 16

No time is set aside for learning

1 —

2 —

A small time is set aside for learning, but only when it's absolutely necessary

3 —

4 —

Time is regularly set aside for learning

5 —

Work Design

Question 17

1	2	3	4	5

Jobs require almost no skill at all; anyone could do them

Jobs require just a few skills, most of which can be learned in a few months

Jobs require many skills which take a long time to learn

Question 18

1	2	3	4	5

People make no important decisions on their jobs; they just do the work as they are told

People make a few important decisions about how their work gets done

People make almost all the important decisions about how their work gets done

Question 19

1	2	3	4	5

People never know how their work turns out

People occasionally know how their work turns out but usually only when they make a mistake

People almost always know how their work turns out, whether it's good or bad

Question 20

1	2	3	4	5

People work alone

People work with a team, but they don't switch jobs

People work with a team, but they don't switch jobs

People work with a team where they regularly switch jobs with one another

Question 21

People do the same thing all the time

1 — 2 — 3 — 4 — 5

People do mostly the same things but occasionally get to do something different

People do a variety of different things

Question 22

People can't do anything their manager does

1 — 2 — 3 — 4 — 5

People can do a few things their manager does

People can do everything their manager does

Question 23

People have no technical skills

1 — 2 — 3 — 4 — 5

People have a few technical skills

People's technical skills are excellent

Question 24

People do only a small piece of an overall task

1 — 2 — 3 — 4 — 5

People do a few pieces of an overall task

People do a whole and complete piece of work

Question 25

Most jobs make no direct contribution to the final product or customer

1 — 2 — 3 — 4 — 5

Most jobs make a small contribution to the final product or customer

Most jobs make a major contribution to the final product or customer

164

Question 26

Most jobs get little or no respect   Some jobs get respect   Most jobs get a great deal of respect

1 — 2 — 3 — 4 — 5

Question 27

There are no opportunities to learn new skills   There are a few opportunities to learn new skills   There are many opportunities to learn new skills

1 — 2 — 3 — 4 — 5

Question 28

People don't do any of the support work for their job (maintenance, set-up, quality control, supply, record keeping, etc.)   People do a little of the support work when they are told to   People frequently do almost all of the support work required by their jobs

1 — 2 — 3 — 4 — 5

Question 29

The pace of work is dictated   People have some flexibility over the pace of their work   People have complete flexibility over the pace of their work

1 — 2 — 3 — 4 — 5

Question 30

People are told what work to do   People can occasionally influence which work they do   People decide which work they want to do

1 — 2 — 3 — 4 — 5

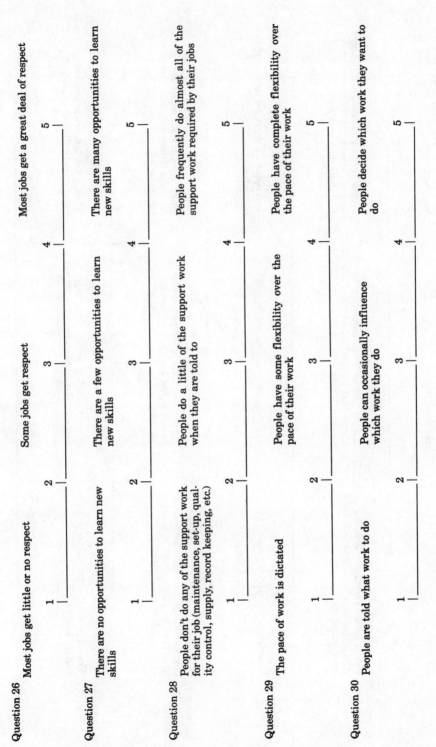

165

Question 31

1	2	3	4	5
People never get involved in problem solving		People occasionally get involved in problem solving		People are frequently involved in problem solving

Question 32

1	2	3	4	5
People have no influence over the things that determine how well their work gets done		People have some influence over the things that determine how well their work gets done		People have a great deal of influence over the things that determine how well their work gets done

Question 33

1	2	3	4	5
Most jobs don't require people to think		Jobs require some thought on people's part		Jobs require a great deal of thought on people's part

Question 34

1	2	3	4	5
Supervisors tell subordinates exactly what to do and then watch to make sure they do it the right way		Supervisors usually tell people how to do things, but are open to a few suggestions		Supervisors explain what needs to be done and let subordinates figure out how to do it

Question 35

1	2	3	4	5
When a problem arises, supervisors step in to solve it		When a problem arises, supervisors will let subordinates solve it if it's not too important		When a problem arises supervisors count on subordinates to solve it

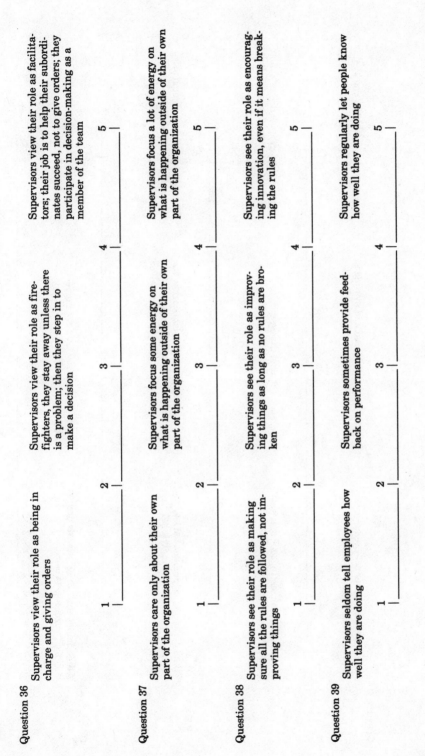

Question 36

1 — Supervisors view their role as being in charge and giving orders

2

3 — Supervisors view their role as firefighters, they stay away unless there is a problem; then they step in to make a decision

4

5 — Supervisors view their role as facilitators; their job is to help their subordinates succeed, not to give orders; they participate in decision-making as a member of the team

Question 37

1 — Supervisors care only about their own part of the organization

2

3 — Supervisors focus some energy on what is happening outside of their own part of the organization

4

5 — Supervisors focus a lot of energy on what is happening outside of their own part of the organization

Question 38

1 — Supervisors see their role as making sure all the rules are followed, not improving things

2

3 — Supervisors see their role as improving things as long as no rules are broken

4

5 — Supervisors see their role as encouraging innovation, even if it means breaking the rules

Question 39

1 — Supervisors seldom tell employees how well they are doing

2

3 — Supervisors sometimes provide feedback on performance

4

5 — Supervisors regularly let people know how well they are doing

Question 40

1	2	3	4	5
Supervisors are never selected or evaluated by their subordinates		Supervisors are selected and evaluated by management with employee input		Supervisors are selected and evaluated by their subordinates

Question 41

1	2	3	4	5
Supervisors use meetings for one-way communication from themselves to employees		Supervisors control the agenda at meetings and allow limited discussion		Supervisors facilitate discussion at meetings on topics chosen by their subordinates

Question 42

1	2	3	4	5
When performance problems arise, supervisors deal with the individual one-on-one		When performance problems arise, supervisors ask for input from subordinates and then take action themselves		When performance problems arise, supervisors help subordinates decide what should be done about it as a team

Question 43

1	2	3	4	5
All decisions regarding rewards are decided by the supervisor		Decisions about rewards are made with some input from subordinates		Decisions about rewards are made by subordinates as a team

Question 44

1 — Supervisors make assignments, schedule work, provide training, review performance and decide on working procedures with no input from subordinates

2 —

3 — Supervisors make assignments, schedule work, provide training, review performance and decide on working procedures with some input from subordinates

4 —

5 — Supervisors help subordinates make assignments, schedule work, provide training, review performance, and decide on working procedures

Question 45

1 — Supervisors speak to higher management on behalf of their subordinates

2 —

3 — Supervisors sometimes allow direct communication between higher management and their subordinates

4 —

5 — Supervisors encourage free and open communication between higher management and their subordinates

Question 46

1 — Supervisors view their presence as essential to the work getting done

2 —

3 — Supervisors feel free to leave their areas for a short period of time without worrying about the work getting done

4 —

5 — Supervisors view their presence as helpful but nonessential to the work getting done

Question 47

1 — Supervisors are selected strictly on the basis of their technical skills

2 —

3 — Supervisors are selected primarily because of their technical skills, but skills in dealing with people are also important

4 —

5 — Individuals will not be selected as supervisors unless they have excellent skills in dealing with people

Organizational Structure

Question 48

There are many levels of management in this organization

1 —— 2 —— 3 —— 4 —— 5

There is an average number of levels of management in this organization

There are few levels of management in this organization

Question 49

Many policies restrict innovation in this organization

1 —— 2 —— 3 —— 4 —— 5

Some policies restrict innovation in this organization

Few policies restrict innovation in this organization

Question 50

Job descriptions limit what most people get involved with here

1 —— 2 —— 3 —— 4 —— 5

Job descriptions are somewhat limiting

Job descriptions either do not exist or do not limit what a person may become involved with

Question 51

Boundaries between departments and/or divisions often interfere with solving joint problems

1 —— 2 —— 3 —— 4 —— 5

Boundaries between departments and/or divisions sometimes interfere with solving joint problems

Boundaries between departments and/or divisions rarely interfere with solving joint problems

Question 52

Meetings seldom occur across levels or between departments in this organization

|— 1 —|— 2 —|— 3 —|— 4 —|— 5 —|

Meetings occur across levels or between departments, but not on a regular basis

Meetings across levels or between departments occur regularly

Question 53

Most people would say that they don't feel as if they were running their own small business within the larger organization

|— 1 —|— 2 —|— 3 —|— 4 —|— 5 —|

Some people would say that they feel as if they were running their own small business within the organization

Many people would say that they feel as if they were running their own small business within the larger organization

Question 54

Work is divided so that each subunit of the organization does only a piece of an overall task; people do not know who completes the task

|— 1 —|— 2 —|— 3 —|— 4 —|— 5 —|

Work is divided so that each subunit does only a piece of an overall task; people know who completes the task

Work is divided so that each subunit of the organization is responsible for making a whole product or providing a complete service

Question 55

Work is divided so that core work (production, customer interaction) is separated from support work (maintenance, record keeping) and belong to different departments

|— 1 —|— 2 —|— 3 —|— 4 —|— 5 —|

Work is divided so that core work and support work are separate, but report to the same supervisor

Work is designed so that core work and support work are integrated

Question 56

1	2	3	4	5
There is no stability among the people who work together on tasks		There is some stability among the people who work together on tasks		There is stability among the people who work together on tasks

Question 57

1	2	3	4	5
No one who performs a task knows how his/her work will affect the work of the next person or the quality of the final product or service		Some people know how their work will affect others or the final production or service		Everyone knows how their work will affect the work of the next person or the quality of the final product or service

Question 58

1	2	3	4	5
People identify more with their function or technology than the product they are making or service they are providing		People identify primarily with their technology or function, but are aware of how the product is made or service is provided overall		People identify primarily with the product or service and seldom identify with one piece of technology or function

ENVIRONMENTAL AGILITY

Environmental Awareness

Question 59

1	2	3	4	5
The organization does not know what its competitors are up to		The organization has only a partial picture of what its competitors are up to		The organization is well aware of what its competitors are up to

172

Question 60

The organization is unaware of technological developments in its area
— 1 —

— 2 —

The organization is somewhat informed about technological developments
— 3 —

— 4 —

The organization is well informed about technological developments
— 5 —

Question 61

The organization is unaware of political/legal/social developments that might affect it
— 1 —

— 2 —

The organization is somewhat informed about political/legal/social developments that might affect it
— 3 —

— 4 —

The organization is well informed about political/legal/social developments that might affect it
— 5 —

Customer Importance

Question 62

The organization is unaware of what customers think about its products or services
— 1 —

— 2 —

The organization has some idea of what customers think about its products or services
— 3 —

— 4 —

The organization is constantly striving to determine what the customer wants and how to meet customer needs
— 5 —

Question 63

Only a few people in the organization talk directly to customers to find out what the organization could do to better serve them
— 1 —

— 2 —

More than a few people talk directly to the customers, but most do not
— 3 —

— 4 —

Many people talk directly to the customers to find out what they could do to better serve them
— 5 —

Question 64

1 — People working on one step of an operation do not regard the people in the next step as their customers. They are not interested in meeting the others' needs

2

3 — People working on one step of an operation will try to meet the needs of the people in the next step only if they are told to do so

4

5 — People working on one step of an operation regard the people in the next step as their customers and try to meet their needs

Question 65

1 — No one knows the standards used by customers to judge the quality of the final product

2

3 — A few specialists know the standards used by customers to judge the final product

4

5 — Everyone knows the standards used by customers to judge the final product and how their own work impacts quality

Proactivity versus reactivity

Question 66

1 — The organization does not respond to changes in its environment unless it is forced to do so

2

3 — The organization sometimes responds to changes in its environment without being forced to do so

4

5 — The organization anticipates changes in its environment and prepares itself for them in advance

Question 67

1 — The organization simply accepts all demands the environment makes and tries to meet them

2

3 — The organization accepts most of the demands the environment makes

4

5 — The organization works actively to change certain demands the environment makes if those demands are likely to do harm to the organization

Structural Flexibility

Question 68

1	2	3	4	5
The organization is unable to adapt to changes because of its existing structure and policies		The organization can adapt to some changes but not to others		The organization can adapt to most changes because its policies and structure are flexible

Technical flexibility

Question 69

1	2	3	4	5
The organization is unable to adopt new technologies or to convert existing technologies to new purposes		The organization can change its technology, but only slightly and with a fair amount of disruption		The organization can adopt new technologies or change existing ones with minimal disruption

Product/Service flexibility

Question 70

1	2	3	4	5
The organization is capable of producing only one product or providing only one service		The organization can produce new products or services if given a large amount of time to do so		The organization can introduce new products or services quickly and easily

COOPERATION

Subunit interdependence

Question 71

Different parts of the organization do not work toward the same goals; there is often destructive conflict between them

Different parts of the organization work together, but not very well

Different parts of the organization work together well; when conflict arises, it is often productive

1   2   3   4   5

Teamwork

Question 72

People look out only for themselves

People look out for themselves and a few others

People work in teams and look out for one another

1   2   3   4   5

Mutual Support

Question 73

People will not help one another if it is beyond their normal duties

People will help one another if they are ordered to do so

People help one another without being told to do so, even if its beyond their normal duties

1   2   3   4   5

Shared Values

Question 74

1	2	3	4	5
No one can state the values behind decisions that are made		A few people know what values are used in making decisions		Everyone can state the values of the organization and how they are used to make decisions

Question 75

1	2	3	4	5
Values, if stated at all, concern only quality and profit		Values mention teamwork, participation, innovation, etc., as important but secondary to quality and profit		Values are stated clearly and place teamwork, participation, innovation, etc, on an equal level with quality and profit

Common rewards

Question 76

1	2	3	4	5
Most people would say that what they do has no effect on rewards *others* receive		A few people would say that how others are rewarded depends on how well they do		Many people would say that what they do affects the amount of rewards *others* receive

Question 77

1	2	3	4	5
Most people would say that they have no influence on the performance ratings their peers receive		A few people would say they have no influence on the performance ratings their peers receive		Many people would say that they have influence on the performance ratings their peers receive

COMMITTMENT/ENERGY

Dedication

Question 78

Few people here feel personally responsible for how well the organization does

Some people here feel personally responsible for how well the organization does

Many people here feel personally responsible for how well the organization does

1 — 2 — 3 — 4 — 5

Question 79

Few people are willing to put in effort above the minimum required to help the organization succeed

Some people are willing to put in effort above the minimum required to help the organization succeed

Many people are willing to put in effort above the minimum required to help the organization succeed

1 — 2 — 3 — 4 — 5

Question 80

Most people slack off when their supervisors are not present

A few people slack off when their supervisors are not present

Almost no one slacks off when their supervisors are not present

1 — 2 — 3 — 4 — 5

Reward Systems

Question 81

People are rewarded the same whether they perform well or not

Some people are recognized for outstandingly good or bad performance

Most people are rewarded based upon their performance

1 — 2 — 3 — 4 — 5

Question 82

People are rewarded for seniority, not for what they know
|— 1 —|

|— 2 —|

People are rewarded primarily for seniority, but also for what they know
|— 3 —|

|— 4 —|

People are rewarded primarily for what they know, not their seniority
|— 5 —|

Question 83

There are large differences in the ways in which managers and their subordinates are rewarded
|— 1 —|

|— 2 —|

There are some differences in the ways in which managers and their subordinates are rewarded
|— 3 —|

|— 4 —|

There are few differences in the ways in which managers and subordinates are rewarded
|— 5 —|

Question 84

Gains in profits due to improvements in performance are not shared with employees
|— 1 —|

|— 2 —|

Gains in profits due to improvements in performance are shared with a few employees
|— 3 —|

|— 4 —|

Gains in profits due to improvements in performance are shared with all employees
|— 5 —|

Question 85

People are rewarded on an individual basis
|— 1 —|

|— 2 —|

People are rewarded primarily as individuals, but some group rewards are also given
|— 3 —|

|— 4 —|

People are rewarded primarily for their teamwork rather than as individuals
|— 5 —|

Information Availability

Question 86

1	2	3	4	5
Little information about the state of the business is shared with employees		Some information about the state of the business is shared with employees		A great deal of information about the business is shared with employees

Question 87

1	2	3	4	5
Most people would say that they did not know what information was being used to make decisions		A few people would say that they know what information was being used to make decisions		Most people would say that they knew what information was being used to make decisions

Question 88

1	2	3	4	5
Managers and technical experts withhold a great deal of information from employees		Managers and technical experts share information on a "need to know" basis		Managers and technical experts share information openly

JOINT OPTIMIZATION

Sociotechnical Balance

Question 89

1	2	3	4	5
Technology is much more important than people in this organization		Technology is somewhat more important than people		Technology and people are of equal importance in this organization

180

Question 90

When new technology is considered the people who will operate it are not considered at all

1 — 2 — 3 — 4 — 5

When new technology is considered, some thought will be given to what work will be like for the people who will operate it

When new technology is considered the people who operate it are intimately involved in decisions regarding its design and development

Question 91

Only a few technical experts understand how the technology works and how to maintain it

1 — 2 — 3 — 4 — 5

Departments of specialists exist who maintain the technology

Most people are capable of performing at least routine maintenance on their equipment

Variance Control

Question 92

Variances (equipment malfunctions or other problems with getting the work done according to standards) are not controlled at their source

1 — 2 — 3 — 4 — 5

Variances are sometimes controlled at their source

Variances are detected and controlled at their source

Question 93

The technology runs poorly (high downtime, low quality)

1 — 2 — 3 — 4 — 5

The technology runs fairly well

The technology runs almost perfectly

Question 94

Most people would say they have no control over the technology they operate

1 ——

2 ——

Most people would say they have some control over the technology they operate

3 ——

4 ——

Most people would say they have complete control over the technology they operate

5 ——

Question 95

Most people would say that they needed help in keeping their technology running properly

1 ——

2 ——

Some people would say that they needed help in keeping their technology running properly

3 ——

4 ——

Few people would say that they needed help in keeping their technology running properly

5 ——

Technological Appropriateness

Question 96

There is a tremendous excess capacity in the technology for the demand being met

1 ——

2 ——

There is a more than adequate excess capacity in the technology for the demand being met

3 ——

4 ——

The technology is well-matched to the demand that is being met

5 ——

Question 97

Technology is poorly understood and maintained by the people operating it

1 ——

2 ——

Technology is barely understood and only adequately maintained by the people operating it

3 ——

4 ——

Technology is well understood and maintained by the people operating it

5 ——

Technological Support for Teamwork

Question 98

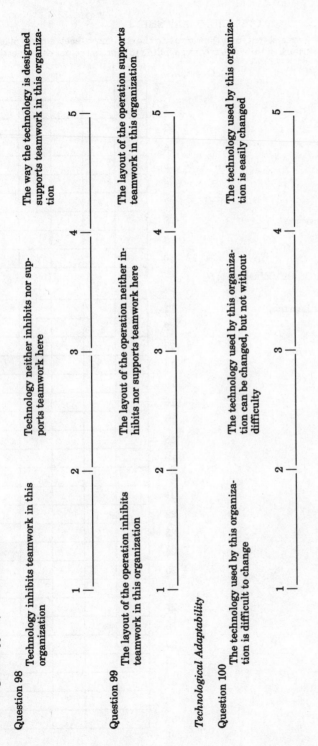

Technology inhibits teamwork in this organization

Technology neither inhibits nor supports teamwork here

The way the technology is designed supports teamwork in this organization

1 — 2 — 3 — 4 — 5 —

Question 99

The layout of the operation inhibits teamwork in this organization

The layout of the operation neither inhibits nor supports teamwork here

The layout of the operation supports teamwork in this organization

1 — 2 — 3 — 4 — 5 —

Technological Adaptability

Question 100

The technology used by this organization is difficult to change

The technology used by this organization can be changed, but not without difficulty

The technology used by this organization is easily changed

1 — 2 — 3 — 4 — 5 —

183

STSAS SUMMARY SHEET

Instructions: To transfer scores from the survey to the summary sheet, simply place a check mark in the column corresponding to your answer for each question.

INNOVATIVENESS	Question #					
Time Orientation	1					
	2					
	3					
	4					
Risk Taking	5					
	6					
	7					
Rewards for Innovation	8					
	9					
	10					

HUMAN RESOURCE DEVELOPMENT/
UTILIZATION

	Question #					
Opportunities for Learning	11					
	12					
	13					
	14					
	15					
	16					
Work design	17					
	18					
	19					
	20					
	21					
	22					
	23					
	24					
	25					
	26					
	27					
	28					
	29					
	30					
	31					
	32					
	33					

HUMAN RESOURCE DEVELOPMENT/
UTILIZATION (Continued)

	Question #					
Supervisory roles	34					
	35					
	36					
	37					
	38					
	39					
	40					
	41					
	42					
	43					
	44					
	45					
	46					
	47					
Organizational structure	48					
	49					
	50					
	51					
	52					
	53					
Work flow structure	54					
	55					
	56					
	57					
	58					

ENVIRONMENTAL AGILITY

	Question #					
Environmental Awareness	59					
	60					
	61					
	62					
	63					
	64					
	65					
Proactivity/Reactivity	66					
	67					
Structural flexibility	68					
Technical flexibility	69					
Product/service flexibility	70					

COOPERATION

Question #

Subunit interdependence   71
Teamwork   72
Mutual support   73
Share values   74
   75
Common rewards   76
   77

COMMITMENT/ENERGY

Dedication   78
   79
   80
Reward systems   81
   82
   83
   84
   85
Information availability   86
   87
   88

JOINT OPTIMIZATION

Sociotechnical balance   89
   90
   91
Variance control   92
   93
   94
   95
Technological appropriateness   96
   97
Tech. support for teamwork   98
   99
Technological adaptability   100

186

REFERENCES

Abernathy, W., Clark, K. & Kantrow, A. The new industrial competition. *Harvard Business Review*, September-October, 1981, 68-81.

Ackoff, R. *Redesigning the Future: A Systems Approach to Social Problems*. New York, Wiley & Sons, 1974.

Ackoff, R. Unpublished speech, University of Pennsylvania, Philadelphia, Pennsylvania, 1972.

Aldrich, H. *Organizations and Environments*. Englewood Cliffs, N.J. Prentice-Hall, 1979.

Argyris, C. *Integrating the Individual and Organization*. New York, Wiley & Sons, 1964.

Argyris, C. Personal versus organizational goals. *Yale Scientific*. February, 1960, 40-50.

Argyris, C. & Schon, D. *Theory in Practice*. San Francisco, Jossey-Bass, 1974.

Asch, S. *Social Psychology*. Englewood Cliifs, N.J., Prentice-Hall, 1952.

Ashby, W. *Design for a Brain*. New York, Wiley & Sons, 1960.

Barnard, C. *The Functions of the Executive*. Cambridge, Massachusetts, Harvard University Press, 1938.

Bartunek, J. & Louis, M. The interplay of organization development and organizational transformation. In W. Pasmore & R. Woodman (Eds.) *Research in Organizational Change and Development*. Greenwich, Connecticut, JAL Press, 1988.

Beckhard, R. *Organization Development: Strategies and Models*. Reading, Massachusetts, Addison Wesley, 1969.

Beckhard, R. & Harris, R. *Organizational Transitions: Managing Complex Change*. Reading, Massachusetts, Addison Wesley, 1977.

Beer, M. *Organization Change and Development*. Santa Monica, California, Goodyear, 1980.

Bell, D. *The Coming of Post-Industrial Society*. New York, Basic Books, 1973.

Bennis, W. *Beyond Bureaucracy*. New York, McGraw-Hill, 1966.

Bennis, W. The artform of leadership. In S. Srivastva (ed.). *The Executive Mind*. San Francisco, Jossey-Bass, 1983.

Bennis, W. The coming death of bureaucracy. *Think*. November-December, 1966, 30-35.

Bennis, W. *Organization Development: Its Nature, Origins and Prospects*. Reading, Massachusetts, Addison Wesley, 1969.

Bennis, W. & Shepard, H. A theory of group development. *Human Relations*, 1956, **9**, (4), 415-438.

Bertalanffy, L. (1950). The theory of open systems in physics and biology. *Science*, 1950, **111**, 23-29.

Bertalanffy, L. Der Organismus als physikalisches System betrachet, *Die Naturwissenschaften*. 1940, **28**, 521-531.

Bion, W. *Experiences in Small Groups and Other Papers*. London, Tavistock, 1961.

Brown, L. *Managing Conflict at Organizational Interfaces*. Reading, Massachusetts, Addison Wesley, 1983.

Bucklow, M. A new role for the work group. *Administrative Science Quarterly*, 1966, 59-78.

Burns, T. & Stalker, G. *The Management of Innovation*. London, Tavistock, 1961.

Bushe, G. *Managerial Resistance in Quality of Worklife Interventions: Its Impact on Evolution*. Unpublished doctoral dissertation, Cleveland, Case Western Reserve University, 1983.

Cherns, A. The principles of sociotechnical design. *Human Relations*, 1976, **29**, 783-792.

Cherns, A. & Wacker, G. Analyzing social systems: The sociotechnical approach. Unpublished, Los Angeles, UCLA Center for Quality of Working Life, 1976.

Chisholm, R. & Ziegenfuss, J. (1987). A review of applications of the sociotechnical systems approach to health care organizations. *Journal of Applied Behavioral Science*, 1987, **22**, (3), 315-328.

Coch, L. & French, J. Overcoming resistance to change. *Human Relations*, 1948, **1**, 512-532.

Cooperrider, D. The egalitarian organization. Unpublished doctoral dissertation, Cleveland, Ohio, Case Western Reserve University, 1985.

Cummings, T. Sociotechnical systems: An intervention strategy. In W. Burke, *Current Issues and Strategies in Organization Development*. New York, Human Science Press, 1976.

Cummings, T. & Griggs, W. Worker reaction to autonomous work groups: Conditions for functioning, differential effects and individual differences. *Organization and Administrative Science*, 1977, 87-100.

Cummings, T. & Srivastva, S. *The Management of Work*. San Diego, University Associates, 1977.

Cummings, T. & Mohrman, S. Self designing organizations: Toward implementing quality-of-work-life interventions. In R. Woodman & W. Pasmore (Eds.) *Research in Organizational Change and Development*. Greenwich, Connecticut, JAI Press, 1985.

Davis, D. & Associates. *Managing Technological Innovation*. San Francisco, Jossey-Bass, 1986.

Davis, S. Culture is not just an internal affair. In R. Kilmann, M. Saxton & R. Serpa (Eds.). *Managing Organizational Culture*. San Francisco, Jossey-Bass, 1985.

Davis, L., Canter, R. & Hoffman, J. Current job design criteria. *Journal of Industrial Engineering*, 1955, **6**, 5-11.

Davis, L. & Taylor, J. Technology and job design. In L. Davis & J. Taylor (Eds.), *Design of Jobs*. Santa Monica, Californis, Goodyear, 1979.

Deal, T. Cultural change: Opportunity, silent killer or metamorphosis? In R. Kilmann, M. Saxton & R. Serpa, *Managing Organizational Culture*. San Francisco, Jossey-Bass, 1985.

Dyer, W. *Team Building: Issues and Alternatives*. Reading, Massachusetts, Addison Wesley, 1987.

Eden, D. Creating expectation effects in OD: Applying self-fulfilling prophecy. In W. Pasmore & R. Woodman (Eds.), *Research in Organizational Change and Development*. Greenwich, Connecticut, JAI Press, 1988.

Elden, M. Sociotechnical systems ideas as public policy in Norway: Empowering participation through worker-managed change. *Journal of Applied Behavioral Science* 1987, **22**, (3), 239-256.

Ellul, J. *The Technological Society*, New York, Knopf, 1964.

Emery, F. Characteristics of sociotechnical systems. Document No. 527, London, Tavistock Institute, 1959.

Emery, F. Some hypotheses about the way in which tasks may be more effectively put together to design jobs. Document No. T.176 London, Tavistock Institute, 1963.

Emery, F. & Trist, E. Analytical model for sociotechnical systems. In W. Pasmore & J. Sherwood, *Sociotechnical Systems: A Sourcebook*. San Diego, University Associates, 1978.

Emery, F. & Trist, E. The causal texture of organizational environments. *Human Relations 1965*, **18**, 21,31.

Emery, M. The search conference. Unpublished, Canberra, Australia, 1982.

Englestad, P. Sociotechnical approach to problems of process control. In F. Bolam (Ed.), *Papermaking Systems and Their Control*. British Paper and Board Makers Association, 1970.

Etzioni, A. *Modern Organizations*. Englewood Cliffs, N.J., Prentice-Hall, 1964.

Festinger, L. *A Theory of Cognitive Dissonance*. Evanston, Illinois, Row and Peterson, 1957.

Foster, M. Developing an analytical model for sociotechnical analysis. Document No. HRC7 and HRC15, London, Tavistock Institute, 1967.

French, W. & Bell, C. *Organization Development: Behavioral Science Interventions for Organization Improvement*. Englewood Cliffs, N.J., Prentice-Hall, 1973.

Friedlander, F. Patterns of individual and organizational learning. In S. Srivastva (Ed.), *The Executive Mind*. San Francisco, Jossey-Bass, 1983.

Friedlander, F. & Brown, L. Organization development. *Annual Review of Psychology*, 1974, **25**, 313-341.

Friedlander, F. & Pickle, H. Components of effectiveness in small organizations. *Administrative Science Quarterly*, 1967, **13**, 289-304.

Fry, R. & Pasmore, W. Strengthening management education. In S. Srivastva (Ed.), *The Executive Mind*. San Francisco, Jossey-Bass, 1983.

Galbraith, J. *Organization Design*. Reading, Massachusetts, Addison Wesley, 1977.

Goodman, P. *Assessing Organizational Change: The Rushton Quality of Work Experiment*. New York, Wiley & Sons, 1979.

Goodman, P. & Associates *Designing Effective Work Groups*. San Francisco, Jossey-Bass, 1986.

Greiner, L. Evolution and revolution as organizations grow. *Harvard Business Review*, 1972, **50**, (4), 37-46.

Gulwosen, J. A measure of work group autonomy. In L. Davis & J. Taylor (Eds.) *Design of Jobs*. Santa Monica, California, Goodyear, 1979.

Hackman, J. & Oldham, G. *Work Redesign*. Reading, Massachusetts, Addison Wesley, 1980.

Hackman, J. The design of work in the 1980's. *Organizational Dynamics*, Summer, 1978, 3-17.

Hancock, W., Macy, B. and Peterson, S. Assessment of technologies and their utilization. In S. Seashore, E. Lawler, P. Mirvis and C. Camman, *Assessing Organizational Change: A Guide to Methods, Measure and Practices*. New York, Wiley & Sons, 1983.

Herzberg, F. One more time: How do you motivate employees? *Harvard Business Review*, 1968 **46**, 53-62.

Herzberg, F., Mausner, B. & Snyderman, B. *The Motivation to Work*. New York, Wiley & Sons, 1959.

Hill, P. *Towards a New Philosophy of Management*. New York, Barnes and Noble, 1971.

Hirschhorn, L. *Beyond Mechanization*. Cambridge, Massachusetts, MIT Press, 1984.

House, R. A path-goal theory of leader effectiveness. In E. Fleishman & J. Hunt (Eds.), *Current Developments in the Study of Leadership*. Carbondale, Illinois, Southern Illinois University Press, 1973.

Hulin, C. & Blood, M. Job Enlargement, individual differences and worker responses. *Psychological Bulletin*, 1968 **69**, 41-55.

Huse, E., *Organization Development and Change*. St. Paul, Minnesota, West Publishing, 1980.

Jayaram, G. Open systems planning. In W. Bennis, K. Benne, R. Chin & K. Corey (Eds.), *The Planning of Change*, New York, Holt, Rinehart and Winston, 1976.

Kahn, R., Wolfe, D., Quinn, R., Snoek, J. & Rosenthal, R. *Organizational Stress: Studies in Role Conflict and Ambiguity*. New York, Wiley & Sons, 1964.

Kanter, R. *The Change Masters*. New York, Simon and Schuster, 1983.

Kanter, R. *Men and Women of the Corporation*. New York, Basic Books, 1977.

Katz, D. & Kahn, R. *The Social Psychology of Organizations*. New York, Wiley & Sons, 1966.

Kerr, S. On the folly of rewarding A while hoping for B. *Academy of Management Journal*, 1975, **18**, 769-783.

Kidder, T. *Soul of a New Machine*. Boston, Atlantic, Little, Brown, 1981.

Kiggundu, M. Limitations to the application of sociotechnical systems to developing countries. *Journal of Applied Behavioral Science*, 1987, **22**, (3), 341-354.

Kilmann, R., Saxton, M. & Serpa, R. *Managing Organizational Cultures*. San Francisco, Jossey-Bass, 1985.

Klien, J. & Posey, P. Good supervisors are good supervisors – anywhere. *Harvard Business Review*, (4), 1986, 125-128.

Kotter, J. *Organizational Dynamics*. Reading, Massachusetts, Addison Wesley, 1978.

Kuhn, *The Logic of Social Systems*. San Francisco, Jossey-Bass, 1974.

Landen, D. & Carlson, H. Strategies for diffusing, evolving and institutionalizing quality of work life in General Motors. In R. Zaeger & M. Rosow (Eds.), *The Innovative Organization*, New York, Pergamon, 1982.

Lawler, E. *Motivation in Work Organizations*. New York, Brooks Cole, 1973.

Lawler, E. *Pay and Organization Development*. Reading, Massachusetts, Addison Wesley, 1981.

Lawrence, P. & Lorsch, J. *Organization and Environment*. Cambridge, Massachusetts, Harvard University Press, 1967.

Levinson, H. Management by whose objectives? *Harvard Business Review* 1970, **48**, (4), 125-134.

Levinson, H. *Organizational Diagnosis*. Cambridge, Massachusetts, Harvard University Press, 1972.

Lewin, K. Action research and minority problems. *Journal of Social Issues*, **2**, 34-46, 1946.

Lewin, K. *Field Theory in Social Science*. New York, Harper & Row, 1951.

Lewin, K. Group decision and social change. In E. Maccoby, T. Newcomb & E. Hartley, *Readings in Social Psychology*. New York, Holt, Rinehart and Winston, 1958.

Lewin, K. *Resolving Social Conflicts*. New York, Harper & Brothers, 1948.

Likert, R. *New Patterns of Management*. New York, McGraw-Hill, 1961.

Lippit, R. The changing leader-follower relationships of the 1980s. *Journal of Applied Behavioral Science*, 1982, **18**, (3), 395-403.

Livingston, J. Pygmalion in management. *Harvard Business Review*, 1969, **47**, (4), 81-89.

Louis, M. Sourcing workplace cultures: Why, when and how. In R. Kilmann, M. Saxton & R. Serpa (Eds.). *Managing Organizational Culture*. San Francisco, Jossey-Bass, 1985.

Mans, C. & Sims, H. Searching for the unleader: Organizational member views on leading self-managed work groups. Unpublished, 1983.

March, J. & Simon, H. *Organizations*. New York, Wiley & Sons, 1958.

Maslow, A. A theory of human motivation. *Psychological Review*, 1943, 370-396.

Maslow, A. *Motivation and Personality*, New York, Harper & Row, 1954.

McGregor, D. *The Human Side of Enterprise*. New York, McGraw-Hill, 1960.

Miewald, R. The greatly exaggerated death of bureaucracy. *California Management Review*. Winter, 1970, 65-69.

Miller, E. Sociotechnical systems in weaving, 1953-1970: A follow-up study. *Human Relations*, 1975, **28**, 349-386.

Miller, E. Technology, territory and time: The internal differentiation of complex production systems. *Human Relations*, 1959, **12**, 245-272.

Morris, B. Internalized oppression: Implications for participative work systems and the liberation of employees. Unpublished doctoral dissertation, Cleveland, Ohio, Case Western Reserve University, 1987.

Mumford, L. *Technics and Civilization*. New York, Harcourt, 1934.

Murray, H. Studies in automated technologies. Unpublished document, London, Tavistock Institute, 1960.

Naisbitt, J. *Megatrends: Ten New Directions Transforming Our Lives*. New York, Warner Communications, 1982.

Noble, D. *America by Design: Science, Technology and the Rise of Corporate Capitalism*. New York, Knopf, 1977.

Noble, D. *Forces of Production: A Social History of Industrial Automation*. New York, Knopf, 1984.

Parsons, T. *The Social System*. New York, Free Press, 1951.

Pasmore, W. The current and future state of sociotechnical systems. Paper presented to the national Academy of Management meeting, Dallas, Texas, 1983.

Pasmore, W. Overcoming the roadblocks in work restructuring. *Organizational Dynamics*, 1982, **10**, 54-67.

Pasmore, W. Turning people on to work. In D. Kolb, J. Rubin & I. McIntyre (Eds.), *Organizational Psychology: A Book of Readings*. Englewood Cliffs, N.J., Prentice-Hall, 1979.

Pasmore, W. & Friedlander, F. An action-research program for increasing employee involvement in problem solving. *Administrative Science Quarterly*, 1982, **27**, 343-362.

Pasmore, W., Morris, B. & Estavez, R. Leadership, organization structure and the quality of work life: An information processing perspective. Unpublished, Cleveland, Ohio, Case Western Reserve University, 1983.

Pasmore, W., Kaplan, M., Cooperrider, D. and Morris B. Performance development. Unpublished, Cleveland, Ohio, Case Western Reserve University, 1983.

Pasmore, W., Petee, J., & Bastian, R. Sociotechnical systems in health care: A field experiment. *Journal of Applied Behavioral Science*, 1987, **22**, (3), 329-340.

Pasmore, W., Srivastva, S. & Sherwood, J. Social relationships and organizational performance: A sociotask approach. In W. Pasmore & J. Sherwood, (Eds.), *Sociotechnical Systems: A Sourcebook*. San Diego, University Associates, 1978.

Pasmore, W., Francis, C., Haldeman, J. & Shani, A. Sociotechnical systems: A North American reflection on empirical studies of the seventies. *Human Relations*, 1982, **35**, (12), 1179-1204.

Pasmore, W. & Sherwood, J. *Sociotechnical Systems: A Sourcebook*, San Diego, California, University Associates, 1978.

Pasmore, W., Shani, A. & Kaplan, M. Sociotechnical systems: An evaluation in an Army data processing facility. Technical report, Army Research Institute, Alexandria, Virginia, 1982.

Pasmore, W. & King, D. Understanding organizational change: A comparative study of multifaceted interventions. *Journal of Applied Behavioral Science*, 1978, **14**, (4), 455-468.

Pava, C. *Managing New Office Technology: An Organizational Strategy*, New York, Free Press, 1983.

Pava, C. Redesigning sociotechnical systems design: Concepts and methods for the 1990s. *Journal of Applied Behavioral Science*, 1986, **22**, (3), 201-222.

Perrow, C. *Complex Organizations: A Critical Essay*, Glenview, Illinois, Scott Foresman, 1972.

Peters, T. & Waterman, R. *In Search of Excellence*. New York, Harper & Row, 1982.

Pfeffer, J. & Salancik, G. *The External Control of Organizations: A Resource Dependency Perspective*. New York, Harper & Row, 1978.

Poza, E. & Markus, L. Success story: The team approach to work restructuring. *Organizational Dynamics*, 1980, **8**, (3), 3-25.

Rice, A. *Productivity and Social Organization: The Ahmedabad Experiment*. London, Tavistock Institute, 1958.

Robbins, S. *Organizational Theory: The Structure and Design of Organizations*, Englewood Cliffs, N.J., Prentice-Hall, 1983.

Roethlishberger, F. & Dickson, W. *Management and the Worker*, Cambridge, Massachusetts, Harvard University Press, 1939.

Rosenthal, R. & Jacobsen, L. *Pygmalion in the Classroom: Teacher Expectation and Pupils' Intellectual Development*. New York, Holt, Rinehart and Winston, 1968.

Rosseau, D. Assessment of technology in organizations: closed versus open systems approaches. *Academy of Management Review*, 1979, 538-542.

Rosseau, D. Technology in organizations: A constructive review and analytic framework. In S. Seashore, E. Lawler, P. Mirvis and C. Camman (Eds.) *Assessing Organizational Change: A Guide to Methods, Measures and Practices*, New York, Wiley & Sons, 1983.

Schein, E. *Organizational Culture and Leadership*. San Francisco, Jossey-Bass, 1985.

Schein, E. *Process Consultation: Lessons for Managers and Consultants*. Reading, Massachusetts, Addison Wesley, 1987.

Schlesinger, L. *Supervision and the Quality of Working Life*. New York, Pergamon, 1983.

Schon, D. *Beyond the Stable State*. New York, Basic Books, 1971.

Schoonhoven, C. Sociotechnical considerations for the development of the space station: Autonomy and the human element in space. *Journal of Applied Behavioral Science*, 1987, **22**, (3), 271-286.

Schumacher, E. *Small is Beautiful*. New York, Harper & Row, 1973.

Segal, H. *Technological Utopianism in American Culture*. Chicago, University of Chicago Press, 1985.

Sherif, M. *In Common Predicament: Social Psychology of Intergroup Conflict and Cooperation*. Boston, Houghton-Mifflin, 1966.

Sherif, M. *Psychology of Social Norms*. New York, Harper, 1936.

Silverman, D. *The Theory of Organizations*. London, Heinemann, 1978.

Simmons, J. & Mares, W. *Working Together*. New York, Knopf, 1983.

Sommerhoff, G. *Analytical Biology*. Oxford, Oxford University Press, 1950.

Stein, B. & Kanter, R. Building the parallel organization: Creating mechanisms for permanent quality of working life. *Journal of Applied Behavioral Science*, 1980, **16**, (3), 371-386.

Stoelwinder, J. & Clayton, P. Hospital organizaton development: Changing the focus from "better management" to "better patient care." *Journal of Applied Behavioral Science*, 1978, **14**, (3), 400-414.

Susman, G. *Autonomy at Work*. New York, Praeger, 1976.

Susman, G. & Chase, R. A sociotechnical analysis of the integrated factory. *Journal of Applied Behavioral Science*, 1987, **22**, (3), 257-270.

Taylor, J. Experiments in work system design: Economic and human results. *Personnel Review*, 1977, **6**, (3), 21-34.

Taylor, J. Long-term sociotechnical systems change in a computer operations department. *Journal of Applied Behavioral Science*, 1986, **22**, (3), 303-314.

Taylor, J. Studies in participative sociotechnical work system analysis and design: Service technology work groups. Paper "CQWL-WP-78-1-B, Los Angeles, UCLA, Center for the Quality of Working Life, Institute of Industrial Relations, 1978.

Taylor, J. & Bowers, D. *The Survey of Organizations*. Ann Arbor, Michigan, Institute for Social Research, 1972.

Thompson, J. *Organizations in Action*. New York, McGraw-Hill, 1967

Tichy, N. & Nisberg, J. When does work restructuring work? Organizational innovations at Volvo and GM. *Organizational Dynamics*, 1976, **6**, 63-80.

Toffler, A. *The Third Wave*. New York, William Morrow and Company, 1980.

Trist, E. The evolution of sociotechnical systems. Toronto, Quality of Working Life Center, Paper #2, 1981.

Trist, E. Quality of working life and community development: Some reflections on the Jamestown experience. *Journal of Applied Behavioral Science*, 1987, **22**, (3), 223-238.

Trist, E. & Bamforth, K. Some social and psychological consequences of the longwall method of coal-getting. *Human Relations*, 1951, **1**, 3-38.

Trist, E., Brown, G. & Susman, G. An experiment in autonomous working in an American underground coal mine. *Human Relations*, 1977, **30**, (3), 201-236.

Trist, E. & Dwyer, C. The limits of laissez-faire as a sociotechnical change strategy. In R. Zaeger & M. Rosow (Eds.) *The Innovative Organization*, New York, Pergamon, 1982.

Trist, E., Higgin, C., Murray, H. & Pollock, A. *Organizational Choice*. London, Tavistock Institute, 1963.

Walters, R. The Citibank project: Improving productivity through work redesign. In R. Zaeger & M. Rosow, *The Innovative Organization*. New York, Pergamon, 1982.

Walton, R. How to counter alienation in the plant. *Harvard Business Review*, 1972, **50**, 70-81.

Walton R. The diffusion of new work structures. *Organizational Dynamics*, 1975, **6**, 3-22.

Walton, R. Innovative restructuring of work. In J. Rosow (ed.), *The Worker and the Job: Coping With Change*. Englewood Cliffs, N.J., Prentice-Hall, 1974.

Walton, R. *Managing Conflict: Interpersonal Dialogue and Third-Party Roles*. Reading, Massachusetts, Addison Wesley, 1987.

Walton, R. The Topeka work system: Optimistic visions, pessimistic hypotheses and reality. In R. Zaeger and M. Rosow (Eds.), *The Innovative Organization*. New York, Pergamon, 1982.

Walton, R. & Hackman, J. Groups under contrasting management strategies. In P. Goodman & Associates (Eds.) *Designing Effective Work Groups*. San Francisco, Jossey-Bass, 1986.

Walton, R. & Schlesinger, L. Do supervisors thrive in participative work systems? *Organizational Dynamics*. Winter, 1979, 25-38.

Weber, M. *The Theory of Social and Economic Organization*. London, Oxford, 1947.

Weick, K. *The Social Psychology of Organizing*. Reading, Massachusetts, Addison Wesley, 1979.

Weiner, N. *The Human Use of Human Beings*. New York, Houghton-Mifflin, 1950.

Whyte, W. *Street Corner Society*. Chicago, University of Chicago Press, 1943.

Woodward, J. *Management and Technology*. London, Her Majesty's Stationery Office, 1958.

Yankelovich, D. *New Rules*. Random House, 1981.

Yukl, G., *Leadership in Organizations*. Englewood Cliffs, N.J., Prentice-Hall, 1981.

Zaeger, R. & Rosow, M. *The Innovative Organization*. New York, Pergamon, 1982.

Zajonc, R. Feeling and thinking: Preferences need no inferences. *American Psychologists*, 1980, **35**, 151-175.

Author Index

196   AUTHOR INDEX

Subject Index

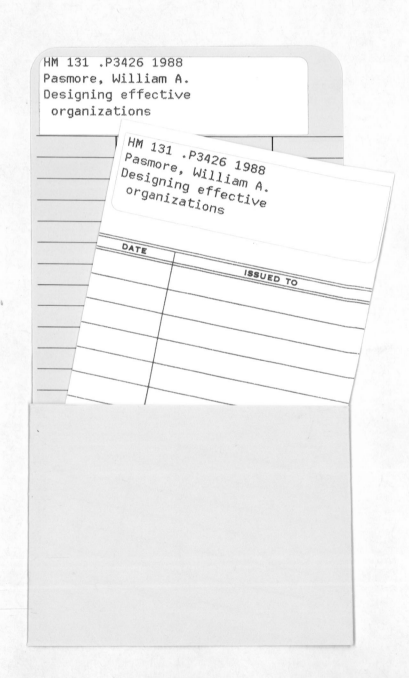